D1348761

FICTION

Contents

PAGE 64

PAGE 108

PAGE 138

FEATURE

FANCY THAT!

TEATIME TREATS

PUZZLES

Laughter&Love!

In spite of a ridiculously early start to their day, these happy stars just love their roles on morning TV!

Bill Turnbull

"Because it covers so many bases, it's the best job in news broadcasting – apart from the time of day," says Bill who aims to present in a friendly and informative way.

Carol Kirkwood

"I enjoy what I do and I hope that comes across. I'm in a very privileged position and get so many amazing opportunities, I never take it for granted."

Louise Minchin

"I love my job and I know I'm really lucky to be in this role. I'm enjoying every minute of *BBC Breakfast* and our new life in the north of England."

Holly & Phil

"We spend a lot of time together and it's nice to see each other outside of work too," says Holly about her beloved *This Morning* co-presenter. "You can't do this show without having a great friendship."

Gino d'Campo

The Italian chef's infectious enthusiasm is something that never fails to put a smile on our faces, too!

Phil Vickery

Daytime TV is the perfect recipe for chef Phil – he first met his wife Fern Britton on a TV set, for starters!

Continued overleaf

Ruth & Eamonn

"We both know what each other is thinking and what we're going to say before we say it," says husband Eamonn. "Ruth's a great co-host and it's been a tremendous privilege to work with someone I love."

Susanna & Kate

"How can you get out of bed at 3.30am? Because you love what you do," explains Susanna.
"I still really, really love it," Kate agrees. "I'm incredibly lucky."

Lorraine Kelly

"I still really love it. I can't imagine not doing it or ever thinking that I have had enough of it. It's the best job in the world," says Lorraine.

Lizzie Webb

"Mad" Lizzie, with bouncy curls and even bouncier feet, helped us to get up and go in the mornings.

Richard & Judy

"The competitive gene doesn't exist for me and Judy, otherwise we never could have presented together for all that time," says Richard of his co-star and wife.

Rustie Lee

Who can forget fabulous *TV-am* chef Rustie? That infectious laugh made us chuckle along with her!

Fern Britton

"I feel very lucky and they were some of the best years of my career," says Fern. Piers Morgan called her on-screen chemistry with Phillip Schofield "a special gift".

Wincey Willis

Wincey always brightened our mornings, however grey the clouds on the weather chart behind her.

Continued overleaf

Anne & Nick

"It was an exciting time," reflects Nick on *TV-am*'s early days, when he specifically requested "girl next door" Anne Diamond as co-presenter. "We were there for another three-and-a-half years. It was very hard work, but hugely enjoyable."

Selina Scott

"The one member of our team who had the glamour to rival the celebs of *TV-am*," says Nick Ross.

Chris & Gaby

"The happiest I've ever been, the tiredest I've ever been, and the most automatic I've ever been," says *The Big Breakfast*'s Chris Evans. Gaby Roslin recalls "being paid to have a great time and to meet incredible people."

Natasha Kaplinsky

"I pleaded with the bosses to rename the programme *Brunch*!" says Natasha, who was always stunning despite early starts.

Roland Rat

Yeaahhhh! The rodent superstar and mates, Errol, Kevin and Glenis, plus brother Reggie were the unlikely solution to dwindling viewer ratings for *TV-am* back in the early 80s.

Jane Corry

The Copper Tree

Their magnificent tree was more than just a beautiful feature in the garden, as this new couple were to find out

I t was the tree I first noticed. Very tall and thick with a vast burnished copper canopy that sheltered the house like a warm pair of arms. Just like Ivan's. "What do you think?" he asked as we stood by the gate, clutching the estate agent's details that flapped in the early autumn wind.

"It's perfect," I replied, watching the way that the top boughs bent towards the upper window; the one that would become our bedroom.

My new husband breathed a sigh of relief. "That's alright, then. For a moment, I thought it was going to be another 'no'."

"It's not just me," I retorted indignantly. "You didn't like the ones I liked, either."

It was true. House hunting is never easy, but when you're doing it for the first time together at an age when many other couples are celebrating their ruby jubilees, it's even more fraught with difficulties.

Ivan was a retired bachelor with a town flat and a microwave. I was a long-term divorcée with an airy maisonette and a kitchen wall covered with grandchildren's scribbles. We both knew what we wanted when it came to selling up and finding a joint home – and it didn't always match.

"We'll be happy here," he said firmly, putting his arm around me. "I know we will."

At first he was right. Of course there were bedding-in issues as I privately called them. Not in "that" department (which ticked along very nicely, thank you very much), but in small things like the cutlery drawer. Ivan carefully placed teaspoons back to back in neat snug silver rows. I chucked them in any old way because years of looking after children and their children and holding down a job, had meant there was little time for niceties.

Apart, of course, from socks. I like to wash them separately in a special laundry bag so they don't get lost. Ivan was so used to wearing mismatches that for the first few weeks of living together, I was convinced he was colour blind.

He didn't like anyone eating in the car, let alone filing their nails. I didn't care for newspapers abandoned casually on the bathroom floor.

Ivan liked to wash up by hand. I pointed out that dishwashers had been made for a reason. You get my drift. He was a Selective Fusser and, I suppose, I was the same.

Continued overleaf

Continued from previous page

Yet none of this mattered – not really – because we loved each other. Often I'd find myself looking at my man over the kitchen table and thinking, *Wow. This is the man I get to go to bed with every night.*

Naturally, that wasn't just it. We made each other laugh too and we both enjoyed walking the hills near our new home and snuggling up on the sofa, reading in the evenings or watching a drama on television. At times, I wondered how on earth I'd got so far in life without Ivan. He said the same, more or less, to me.

Then came the call about the tree. "Mrs Collins?" said a voice. "This is the tree surgeon. I've had a cancellation for tomorrow. I can be there first thing in the morning to cut it down."

What on earth was he talking about? For a start, I'm *not* Mrs Collins. Ivan and I had decided right at the beginning, that marriage wasn't on the cards. I'd been bruised that way before and Ivan had been to too many weddings that had ended in separate address book entries.

More important was the tree.

"Which tree?" I demanded hotly, realising as I spoke that there was only one to speak of. Our new home didn't have a very big garden. The rest of it was mainly shrubs and a small patch of lawn; just enough for us to sit out on next summer, we'd told ourselves. "What I mean is," I added quickly, "what makes you think that it has to come down?"

"Mr Collins booked me," said the voice at the other end in a tone that suggested this wasn't the first time he'd had a foliage marital dispute. "He called me out to look at it and I have to say that its roots might pose a problem to your house foundations."

"*Might* or *would*?" I insisted.

The tree surgeon hesitated. Only for a second but it was enough. "It's difficult to say but it's always wise to err on the side of caution."

Well, he would say that, wouldn't he? Otherwise all tree surgeons would be out of business. Forget about the foundations to a house – what about the foundations of a non-marriage?

It's got to come down," said Ivan firmly when he got back from the DIY shop with some hardboard to block in a tiny gap in the skirting board that didn't really need filling in.

"You're just fussing as usual," I shot back. "I love that tree. It's been there for years – you can't just tear it down like that. Besides, it's why I wanted to buy the house."

"Don't be so childish." Ivan's voice sounded irritated in a way I'd never heard before. "If the tree doesn't come down, we won't *have* a house."

"Fine." I flung on my jacket and grabbed my overnight bag. "Then you won't have me either."

It took a while to reach my daughter's and when I did, no-one was in. So I sat in her garden and waited. I thought of the tree and how long it had been there. I thought of the spoons that had to be placed back to back and I thought of my first husband who had been so controlling and I wondered how on earth I had got myself into this mess.

I looked at my watch and realised this was the time that Ivan and I usually took a stroll in the hills, his arm around my shoulders, while we talked books or music or whatever was going on in our heads.

"Granny!" called out a little joyous voice. A small bundle threw herself into my arms, closely followed by my daughter, with a what-are-you-doing-here? expression on her face. "Look what I made at school today!"

She held up a large sheet of white paper for inspection with a proud beam on her face. I glanced at it and promptly burst into tears. "It's called leaf printing, granny," said my youngest grandchild, her little brow furrowing. "Don't you like it?"

"I think," said my daughter shepherding me inside, "that granny needs a nice cup of tea."

At least go back for some clean clothes," urged my daughter after a week during which I had refused to text or ring Ivan on the grounds that he had done neither to me. So I did. I chose a time when I knew Ivan would be at the council rubbish tip because that's what he did every Wednesday at precisely 2pm after lunch. However, as soon as I parked outside the house that was meant to be our new home, I realised two things. First, Ivan's car was in the drive. Secondly, the tree was still there.

"I couldn't do it," he said, opening the door before I had a chance to slide my key in the lock. "Not without your say-so."

I nodded. "My daughter says I ought to tell you something." Taking his hand, I led him to the tree and ran my finger along its cool, grainy bark before closing my eyes

Why is it that children eventually become so much wiser than their parents?

It wasn't until I'd had something much stronger, that I came out with the full story. Why is it that children eventually become so much wiser than their parents?

"Ivan should have talked to you first," agreed my daughter. "But you also need to listen, Mum. He's not the only one who's set in his ways, you know. In fact, from what you've told me, the tree argument is just what you need to really get to grips with each other. After all, it's not as though you've been together that long, is it?"

Point taken. Silver internet dating has a lot to answer for. Even so, a woman has her pride, especially when she knows that she's right!

and allowing the memories to seep in.

Together, in unspoken agreement, we sat on the damp leaves that had begun to fall on the ground. "When I was a child, we had an apple tree. It was the only tree in the garden, just like this one. It had a low branch which was perfect for sitting on and reading. Then one day, I came home from school and it had gone. The neighbours complained it affected their light so my parents had it cut down."

I paused to check Ivan was still listening. He was. "That was the year that my parents got divorced," I added. "After that, nothing ever really felt secure again."

His fingers were beginning to lace into

Continued overleaf

mine. "I should have told you something too." He closed his eyes briefly. "I'm not really a bachelor. I got married once when I was very young, more than forty years ago. Two weeks after we got married, I came home to find she had gone. Just like that. All she left was a note with one word. It just said *Sorry.*

"I moved away and started a new life. I've never told anyone else this because I felt so embarrassed." His eyes met mine. "A psychologist might say it's why I don't like feeling out of control."

We sat under the tree for some time afte r that, telling each other all the little things that a couple usually tell each other over the months or years of a usual courtship – if there's such a thing nowadays. By the time we finished, it was getting dark and a wind was whipping up.

"You're cold," he said, putting his arm around me. "Shall we go inside?"

I n the morning, when we woke, half the tree was gone. The other half was lying on our neighbour's garden.

"Someone could have been killed," I whispered appalled, waiting for Ivan to say *I told you so.*

Instead he gave me a big warm hug. "But they weren't, were they?"

Luckily, we have very understanding neighbours. In fact, the following year,

they came to the ceremony. My youngest granddaughter wore a bridesmaid dress even though it wasn't that kind of wedding. "It's a celebration," explained Ivan as he passed me the shovel. I pushed it into the earth, feeling it sink deep down.

Then my eldest grandson, who's studying horticulture at college, picked up the new tree that we'd bought from the garden centre. The type where the roots aren't likely to affect the foundations, apparently. Each grandchild – all seven of them – then flung some earth on top before Ivan finally patted it firmly in place.

"It's not as big as the old one," remarked my daughter thoughtfully, "but it will grow."

Ivan's hand squeezed mine. We both knew what the other was thinking. We'll grow old together too, but only if each one of us thinks carefully before dislodging the other's roots.

"Anyone for tea and cake?" suggested my son-in-law hopefully.

We went inside where the teaspoons lay neatly, back to back in the cutlery drawer and the youngest grandchild began to practise her dextrous skills on the kitchen walls with a wax crayon that belonged to her older sister.

"Don't do that," groaned her father.

"It's alright," said Ivan quickly. "We're going to redecorate soon anyway."

And that's when I knew we were going to be all right, after all.

5 Moments To Remember

Author Jane Corry shares the highlights of her writing life

1

◆ **My first highlight was at the age of eight when I had a letter published in the girls' comic, *June & Schoolfriend*. I will never forget my excitement at reading it in print while sitting on the back door step before going to class.**

◆ I had written about going to the Lord Mayor's fancy dress party for children in London. We lived next door to the mayor of Harrow at the time. His own daughter was grown up so he'd taken me along with another little girl, who was also his neighbour. I'd wanted to go as a princess but my mother dressed me up as a fairy prince instead as she had a suitable black cloak! The printed article helped to make up for the disappointment.

2

◆ **My next writing step was winning a poetry competition run by our local paper (the *Harrow Observer*) when I was 17. My poem was about a candle. I was stunned – it almost felt as though this was happening to someone else.**

3

◆ On my 19th birthday, I had my first article published in the university magazine. I distinctly recall walking across the campus, steps springing in the icy wintry grass! Two years later, I wrote a feature about an arts exhibition for the *Western Mail* in Cardiff where I trained as a journalist. I'll never forget seeing someone read it on the train. I wanted to say, "That's me!"

4

◆ **The biggest thrill was last September when my agent rang to say that Penguin had accepted my first psychological thriller, *My Husband's Wife*. My novel is set in the world of law, love and prisons. I'm still pinching myself because it has always been my dream to have the Penguin logo next to my name!**

5

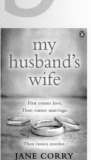

my
husband's
wife

First comes love.
Then comes marriage.

Then comes murder.

JANE CORRY

Secret Valentine

Sometimes a potential romance requires a little mischief and interference to get things started…

By Catherine Howard

Emma passed a card across the reception desk. "It's for Phil Jones," she whispered.

"You're joking!" Liz gasped. "I didn't think he was your type."

"He isn't," Emma agreed. "I thought a Valentine might loosen him up. I'm going to put it in his in-tray."

The card showed a man wearing baggy clothes and slippers. Inside was the same man, only this time smartly dressed and wearing a smile. The caption read, *Get smart – you've got an admirer.*

Liz frowned and pushed the Valentine card away.

"Sending somebody a card when you don't like them is cruel. You know his fiancée broke off their engagement, two months before the wedding."

"In that case," said Emma wickedly, "why don't *you* send him one? You've been sweet on him for ages."

"I have not!" she exclaimed.

Emma raised her right eyebrow.

"It's just a laugh, Liz. Don't be so serious all the time. You're as bad as him."

Liz glanced at her colleague's desk where four Valentine's cards competed for attention. Since breaking up with her boyfriend four months ago, she hadn't had so much as a date. Emma, on the other hand, was always being asked out but kept saying no. She said she had a steady boyfriend, but Liz had never seen him.

She wondered if getting a card would upset Phil, but she needn't have worried. When he arrived the next morning, an hour late, he strode in, a broad smile on his face.

"Morning, ladies," he said.

Liz stared at him. He was wearing smart new clothes and he'd had his hair

Continued overleaf

He looked so wretchedly disappointed at her news that Liz's heart went out to him

Be my Valentine.

Continued from previous page

trimmed. The difference was amazing.

"See," whispered Emma. "All he needed was a confidence boost. He's like a different man."

"Yes," hissed Liz, "because he thinks a pretty woman, i.e. you, fancies him."

She bumped into Phil later when she needed some photocopying. As soon as he saw Liz, he smiled.

"You seem happy today," she said.

"I am." He chuckled. "All because of a Valentine. It gave me such a boost. All I need now is the courage to ask the lovely E out on a date."

Liz had heard enough. "Good luck," she said, and almost ran to the stairs. The photocopying could wait.

Back at reception, she told Emma what had happened.

"He's about to ask you out!"

But Emma wasn't listening.

"My boyfriend just called – from Spain." She paused dramatically. "He's coming home later today! For good. Isn't that wonderful?"

"Yes and I'm very happy for you, but what about Phil? When he finds out the Valentine's card was a joke, he'll be upset."

"He'll be fine," replied Emma, a faraway look in her eyes. "There's so much I need to do. Can you cover for me if I go early?"

"Fine, go on," sighed Liz.

Emma hugged her.

"Thanks, hun. Before I go, can you tell Phil what happened? It will be easier coming from you…"

With a heavy heart Liz trudged into Phil's office and came out with it.

"That Valentine's card. Emma's going steady – there's no point asking her out."

"Oh. I see."

He looked so wretchedly disappointed that Liz's heart went out to him.

"Don't be too upset," she said. "She's been seeing him for ages. I'm sure she'd –"

"That's not why I'm disappointed." He paused. "I thought you'd sent the card."

"*Me?*" Liz blinked.

"Yes. It was signed E, for Elizabeth. You are Elizabeth Mansfield, aren't you?"

"Well, yes, I am – but everyone calls me Liz. The card was from Emma."

"I see. Emma's very pretty – but you're warm and funny and…"

Liz interrupted him. "Do you have any plans for dinner?"

When she got back to reception, Emma was ready to leave.

"Was Phil very upset?" she asked.

Liz blushed. "Not really." She pointed at the name plate on the desk which read Elizabeth Mansfield. "He thought *I'd* sent the card. We're going out to dinner."

"That's wonderful!" As Emma left, she uncrossed her fingers. Liz and Phil were made for each other. All they needed was a gentle push… which was why she'd signed the card "E" in the first place.

THE AUTHOR SAYS…

"I love writing Valentine stories and try to write some every year. Each time I write about Valentine cards I secretly hope that one day soon, somebody might send me a card…"

FANCY THAT!

Fascinating facts about **the air we breathe**

✦ Air is a mixture of nitrogen (78%), oxygen (21%), water vapour, dust particles and other gases (1 %).

✦ About 20% of the world's population breathes air contaminated from industrial processes.

✦ There are 3 billion insects passing over your head in the average summer month in Britain.

✦ If there was no air we'd be bombarded by meteors – the friction of our atmosphere burns them into small harmless fragments.

Air pollution is not a new thing; in 1952 the Great Smog of London caused almost 8000 deaths!

✦ Our lungs are about the size of two footballs, yet when stretched out their total surface area would cover a tennis court.

✦ Although plants and trees provide oxygen and cut down on carbon dioxide in the air, most of the oxygen in our atmosphere actually comes from the huge abundance of algae in the oceans.

✦ A commercial jet plane has an average cruising speed of 550mph.

✦ Alpine swifts soar over Europe and Africa and are truly at home in the air. Surviving on insects, they can stay aloft for seven months at a time.

✦ Insects that migrate long distances hitch rides on fast winds that move in front of storm fronts, as it's more energy efficient than flapping wings.

✦ Our lungs can hold 4-6 litres of air on average, though we use only a small portion of this with each breath.

80% of lung diseases are due to air pollution from motor vehicles

✦ Bacteria has been found thriving 4 to 6 miles above Earth's surface and can ride the winds from continent to continent.

Knit Two Together!

Tess's wonderful idea of rehabilitating both Jack and
her gran is in danger of coming off the needles…

By Jo Styles

Tess frowned as she watched her gran, Lizzie, sitting listlessly in front of the TV.

How long had it been now since she'd left her bungalow? No matter how many times she cajoled her gran, she refused to budge. Even her meals were being delivered now.

She saw Lizzie's gaze stray to the picture on the bookcase. Grandad stared out longingly from it, as if he missed them both as much as they missed him.

"So shall I go and fetch him in for a visit, then?" Jess asked. "I'm trying to cure his anxiety by leaving him alone for gradually longer spells of time in my car."

"He had a skin condition," Jess explained. "It's fine now. He's just a bit bald in places."

Jack stood trembling as if a blast of chilly wind had caught him by surprise. Jess stood furiously wishing. Wishing her gran would at least smile at him. Wishing she'd cheer up just a tiny bit.

"He needs a coat," Lizzie said suddenly. "I could knit him one."

She frowned, likely thinking of Grandad. His face had always glowed with pride when he wore one of the jumpers she'd made. In the picture on the bookcase he wore a big blue cable-knit sweater with a collar that stretched right up over his chin.

"Yes, that's a good idea," she mused.

"Oh my word," Lizzie said, peering at his back. "What's the matter with his fur?"

Lizzie blinked at her "Sorry, love?"

"Jacquard Jabberwocky."

"Did his last owners really call him that?"

"I shortened it to Jack when I got him. I'll fetch him in before he starts chewing my car seats again."

Jack was Jess' Chihuahua. He had liquid brown eyes, huge bat ears and a tongue that licked everything: carpet, furniture… and Lizzie's hands.

She jolted back in alarm.

"He doesn't bite, Gran," Jess said.

"Well, he does – but only my furniture legs and my cushions."

Jack did a little dance, his rear end wriggling under the force of his lashing tail. He decided to lick Lizzie's slippers.

"Oh my word," she said, peering at his back. "What's the matter with his fur?"

"I'll knit him a little coat. He's so tiny, it won't take long."

Wonderful, Jess thought, as Jack licked the fireplace then the side of the wicker bin. *Only that won't get you back on your feet and out of the house, will it?*

"His previous owner bought Jack to use as a furry clutch bag." That was what Elsa at the dogs' home had told Jess. "Dogs aren't accessories," she'd added, her eyes flashing in annoyance. "Do you know why they brought him here? Do you know why they threw him out?"

At her gran's bungalow the next evening, Jess chewed her lip thoughtfully.

The coat her gran had knitted for her

Continued overleaf

Continued from previous page

little visitor at the speed of an express train was thick, green and white. It slipped over Jack's head easily. Lizzie fastened the little knitted strap around his middle and buttoned him up. He stood on the sofa next to her, eyes bright, looking as proud as Grandad ever had.

"Well now," Lizzie said cheerfully. "Don't you look handsome?"

Jack posed for another ten seconds. Then he started to quiver, then to shake. Then he exploded like a mini firework. He flung himself at Lizzie's cushions,

"No…no," Lizzie interrupted. "It might be that wool making him itch." She started hunting through the forlorn scraps left in her knitting cupboard. "He needs something softer, the poor little mite."

"Jack's previous owners used to leave him on his own for hours during the day when he was a puppy," Elsa had explained at the dogs' home. "They used to take him clubbing too. They'd show him off to their friends then dump him in their car until three in the morning. No wonder his friendly licking turned to anxious chewing."

"Look at my gran's face, Jack. She really needs to feel good about something…"

thrashing between them like a demented snake trying desperately to free himself of his jacket. Finally he left it behind like a shed skin.

Elsa's voice echoed in Jess' head.

"Well, for a start they got rid of him because he refused to wear clothes. He didn't want to dress as Elvis at their fancy dress party. He refused to wear a spider costume for Hallowe'en. They thought there must be something wrong with him."

"Oh," Lizzie said. "Oh…" She sniffed, her bottom lip trembling as she picked up Jack's discarded coat from the settee.

It was the first piece of her knitting she'd ever had rejected.

"He's just a bit…highly strung," Jess excused before sighing at her little dog. *Couldn't you just like it? Couldn't you just make her happy?*

"I'll have to try again," Lizzie said.

"No, Gran. Really, I don't think he'll wear…"

Gran's next coat would have shocked the most outrageous of night clubbers. It was nine different colours. It was gloriously soft, but it had been made out of odds and ends of wool left over from Grandad's jumpers.

During his next visit, Jack, wearing his techni-coloured dream-coat, backed across the lounge.

"He doesn't like the colour," Lizzie said. "I'm only trying to keep you warm until your coat grows back, sweetheart," she told Jack.

Stop reversing, Jess screamed in her head, as he backed into the coffee table's leg, bumped off it and hit the TV stand.

Please like it. Please. Look at my gran's face, Jack. She needs you to like it. She really needs to feel good about something right now.

He carried on backing up. She half expected a beep, beep, beep noise to start up while a robotic voice announced

"Caution. This Chihuahua is reversing".

He reversed into the sofa, ducked his head and reversed himself right out of his coat.

"I knew he hated it," Lizzie said resignedly. "It's such a nasty combination of colours."

"Gran, he's a *dog*," Jess said. "He doesn't get up every morning and colour-code his dog biscuits."

"I must have some more wool tucked away upstairs somewhere," Lizzie replied as if she hadn't heard a word. "I wonder what colours he likes?"

Dogs aren't people," Elsa from the dogs' home had said. 'They're pack animals. They need to know their place. Jack never knew his; that's why he started ripping his last owners' house apart. I mean he might be tiny but he can do his share of damage.

"You might lose some furniture while you're rehabilitating him. Are you prepared for that?'

How Jess had shrunk under Elsa's stern gaze. Now she shrank under her gran's for an entirely different reason. After two weeks her gran had knitted Jack a total of six coats. All had been rejected.

"They're just the wrong size, the wrong fit or the wrong colour," Lizzie had reasoned stoically.

Today, Jack sat licking the hearth rug. He looked round to check with Jess.

"No," she said quietly. "No."

He switched to licking his own paw instead. Then he peered at the television screen. *Did that need licking? Did the pouffe?* she could see him thinking.

"No," Jess said firmly.

He didn't move. He just sat quietly, his eyes fixed on her.

Lizzie held up coat number seven.

"It's lovely, Gran," Jess said. "But you
Continued overleaf

must be out of wool by now." She opened up the cupboard and stared inside. Balls of wool lay there stacked into colour-coded piles. "Oh… you found lots more."

"No," Lizzie said. "I bought lots more." Jess whirled about.

"You've been *out*? You went to the wool shop? But that's a bus ride away, Gran. That's right the other side of town."

Her gran frowned.

"Well, of course I went out." She said it in a scandalised tone as if she hadn't been sitting like a frozen monument for three whole months now, her only company all day her photo album and her television.

"I went to see Mrs Clarke at the wool shop," she said. "Then I went to visit

Jack," she told him gently. "It's not to dress you up. You don't need to be anything else here except a dog."

In her gran's lounge as Lizzie put on his coat, Jack looked at Jess. He twitched, he squirmed, he whimpered deep in his throat. Was he remembering wearing bunny ears or being dressed like a disco king? Was he recalling how confused he felt as he was passed around like a handbag before being abandoned for hours?

"There now," Lizzie said.

His new coat was taupe with a soft, wide, ribbed roll neck. It was his most tasteful outfit yet.

Hate it, Jess willed him. *She needs you*

"You put me to shame, Jack. Here I am sitting in the dark when it's a lovely day"

Millie Jackson. We always used to swap knitting patterns. She has a computer. She prints out patterns all the time. Then I went to see Anne Smithers. She has a little dog. He has a lovely blue coat – it's waterproof."

Jess held her breath, feeling doomed as Elsa's words came booming into her head. "Poor Jack will need hours of training. He'll need patience and understanding."

Jess had started to teach him not to fret when he was alone, not to let his licking turn into chewing. She'd taught him to sit and to stay. For the last two weeks at night when he was sleepy, she'd draped a little hanky over him so he'd learn to accept the weight of the cloth.

"Gran's coat is just to keep you warm,

to hate it this time. She needs to knit. She needs to hunt down new patterns and go and see her friends. She'll get stuck here again, Jack.

His tail twitched so did his huge ears. He whined and looked at her for guidance. He was a member of a pack now after all and Jess was his trusted leader.

Then suddenly he flopped down… and yawned.

"Oh…" Lizzie said, blinking at him in shock. "Oh… he likes it." Her disappointment filled the room from corner to corner.

"Gran," Jess said in panic. "We… we… should take him out." She gave a little whistle. The walkies whistle she'd taught Jack at home.

He charged towards the door then

She remembered the dogs' home and how Elsa had waved a handful of adoption forms at her.

Why do you want a dog?" she'd demanded.

"I…I lost my grandad a few months ago," Jess had replied quietly. "My grandparents as good as brought me up. Everything feels so empty without him."

You're not suitable, she expected Elsa to snap before she said another word. *Dogs aren't for filling holes in your life. They're not emotional Polyfilla.*

Instead Elsa sighed.

"So you need a little rescue dog, do you?" she'd asked.

L izzie gazed down at the little dog as his tail thrashed excitedly.

"You put me to shame, Jack," she said. "Here I am sitting in the dark, when it's a lovely spring day outside."

She smiled bravely at Jess. "I don't need a reason to go out, love, do I? I can just go. Come on; let's take Jack for a walk before you take him home. We always used to go for walks in the sunshine with your grandad."

As Lizzie hunted for her own coat, Jess clipped on Jack's lead. She petted his huge ears.

"Well done, Jack," she whispered. "You're not a toy or a handbag, I promise. You're a real dog, a proper dog – but you're not just any old dog, Jack. You're a rescue dog."

stood in front of it, his tail swishing madly.

Give Gran a bigger reason to go out, Jess thought.

"He… he can meet all your friends now they've heard all about him. He loves people, Gran."

Lizzie gazed at the picture of Grandad in his cable knit sweater, smiling at her.

She's going to say no, Jess thought. *She thinks even having one moment of happiness is wrong without Grandad.*

THE AUTHOR SAYS...

"I met an elderly lady and her little dog. 'He's my daughter's,' she told me. 'Oh, do you just take him out then?' I asked. 'Oh no,' she said. 'He takes *me* out.'"

An Easter Gift

It's been a long journey, but at last the darkness has lifted and a new light has come into our lives

By Gabe Ellis

Lying in bed, I concentrate on the jackdaws shouting at each other, the spattering of rain on the window and the creaking of the trees outside. I lie perfectly still, perfectly numb; no more tears, and even my rage is exhausted. It has been eight days since I lost my baby, eight days since I had to leave the hospital empty-handed, my belly and my heart just as empty and aching. It was Easter Monday.

The jackdaws keep bickering, my husband turns over next to me but I don't move. Sounds of distant traffic remind me that life continues, even though that seems impossible.

I remember that drive home from the hospital, watching a succession of buildings, cars, trees and families, neither of us able to talk. I couldn't believe that the world looked so normal when surely everyone should have been in mourning, everywhere should have shut down. Tears slipped endlessly down my face and my hands cradled my belly, unable to believe he was gone. My beautiful boy.

There was a problem when his skull formed, they said. Everything else was perfect, but there was no way he could survive once born, there wouldn't even be a way to operate. Even now, listening to the sounds of the world waking up, my brain cannot accept that there was nothing that could be done. I've been angry at the doctors, angry at my husband and black with rage at my powerlessness, but now it's just numb. He's gone.

Easter is supposed to be a time of new life, of birth and fruition. It was too cruel to tell me that there's nothing they can do, that my child can't be saved, that for me Easter will be a time of indescribable loss.

Wherever he is, my lost baby Louie, I've gone with him.

It's been one year now, one year today. Dave has been especially concerned this week, watching his wife for signs of depression as the date drew near. Not surprising, given how close he came to losing me a few months ago.

I would never have thought of myself as suicidal, certainly not one for dramatic gestures or calls for help, but it just got too much; I felt as if I would never stop

Continued overleaf

Continued from previous page

hurting and that it would simply be better for everyone if I slipped away. Since losing Louie, half of me has never come back anyway. It's like he got cut adrift on an endless ocean and when he slipped over that horizon, some essential part of me went, too.

Whenever I stand on the shore, gazing at the line between sea and sky, I feel as if he's just there, just out of reach.

Dave and I nearly split up earlier this year. I couldn't take being responsible for his pain as well as my own, tried telling him to go, to leave. I couldn't handle the guilt at not being able to keep Louie, not being able to fix our baby. As his mother, I should have been able to make everything better, shouldn't I?

Poor Dave, he's never blamed me, never done anything except try to support me, his eyes filled with pain, saying the right things, reminding me how the doctors assured us there was nothing we'd done wrong, that it was *just one of those things.*

What a ridiculous phrase. My happiness crushed, my heart aching, our marriage almost destroyed and it's *just one of those things.*

Like when people ask us so casually when we're planning to have children, a twinkle in the eye as they tease us, and I want to scream at them – but you can't, you can't tell them you lost your baby because it would make them uncomfortable.

Dave's mum invited us for Easter lunch but I couldn't go, I needed to go to the sea with a flask of coffee and all my pain and talk to my baby. Alone.

Two years have passed. Another Easter Monday has come around, with no black armbands or national mourning, only chocolate eggs in bright wrappings.

I still believe that everything happens for a reason, even if we can't see it at the time. I know that there was a reason we couldn't keep Louie, that however hard it was to let him go so soon, there was a reason. People tell me it's good to have such faith, but it's not a choice – it's just something I am sure of.

It still makes me ache when I see mothers with their children, when I catch that clinical smell of hospitals or see an ultrasound scan, remembering his shadowy movements. At those times, my hands unconsciously hold my belly, trying to connect.

Sometimes, a piece of music will catch me unawares and I need to run away, to cry and shout and rant until I hiccup with the magnitude of my grief and the mess it has left in its wake.

Other mothers have babies they don't even care for, women who didn't even want to have children, and their babies are healthy and fit and fine. It's not fair…

In the great scheme of things I know it will all come good but it hurts so much. I can't believe I've any tears left, it has exhausted me these last two years.

I need to talk to Dave, really talk to

him, but I'm afraid of all that grief, whether it can ever ease or whether it will eventually consume us.

He tactfully changes channels if baby-related shows are on, squeezes my hand in solidarity when people talk enthusiastically about babies, and I know we're in it together. There was the doctor and the two of us when Louie was born; we saw him and loved him and only Dave shares that with me.

Today is Louie's third birthday. It is the first time I have been able to see this not as the day he died, but the day he was born. Instead of *he would have been,* I suddenly feel that he *is* three today – he might not be here with me, in my arms, but today he is three.

I'm at the beach today, toasting Louie's fourth birthday with a flask of coffee, but I'm not alone. Dave is beside me on the blanket, gazing at the sea, smiling quietly to himself.

Asleep between us is Matty. He is just over three months old, and is the most beautiful baby I have ever seen. His name chose itself the moment we knew we were expecting – it comes from Matthew, and means "a gift from God".

He would have been conceived just around Easter last year, a time for new beginnings, and he was born on New Year's Day – all of which somehow seems completely inevitable.

I was filled with an amazing warmth that stayed with me long after I awoke

This year it's been easier to breathe. I have spent less time thinking about the missed milestones of his first smiles, his first steps, all the normal things that we never got to enjoy. I have started to feel as if this Easter, I am coming back to life.

There is another reason for this, perhaps: the dream I had last night. I dreamt with absolute clarity that I saw Louie, a three-year-old boy with shining eyes and a broad smile, telling me fantastic things. He didn't seem to use words but I knew him, I understood everything and I was filled with an amazing warmth that stayed with me long after I awoke. I have a feeling of contentment, almost excitement; it was so wonderful to see him.

Stroking his soft, soft cheek, I glimpse the profile of his brother that I recall so clearly from the ultrasound scans. This time, I can stroke and love and care for this baby, and Dave and I have already agreed that no baby can have too many cuddles, especially not this one.

With my arms around my husband and my sleeping child, I wish Louie a happy birthday and send a silent *thank you* to the horizon for this most wonderful of gifts.

THE AUTHOR SAYS...

"Usually, my writing is fiction, but this draws on my own experience of losing a baby six years ago. I hope it helps other mums and speaks to many readers."

Freedom Walks

The moors, Malta, west coast beaches – now at last she had the time to revisit all her favourite places

By Rose Layland

When she thought about it, there was a lot to be said for her present situation.

After years of deadlines, demands, the needs of family, it was a shock to find she now had no responsibilities. The days stretched empty before her. She could go where she pleased. Do what she pleased.

Today? Easy. I'll drive to Exmoor, walk from Tarr Steps towards Withypool. Have a cream tea at Winsford.

It was spring and the young buds hung like green rain above the tawny river. Songbirds vied with each other in the exhilaration of the season. She emerged from the crowding trees into rough turf and bracken where she saw the brilliant flash of a cock pheasant racing for cover.

There were rich, tangy scents from old themselves in rich mosses and lichens.

On the tops she came across wild ponies, some big with foal, which paused in their rhythmic tugging and nibbling to regard her with handsome eyes. Their russet coats were shaggy with moulting hair, which would be seized by nesting birds.

Not for the first time, she reflected that in nature nothing is wasted.

Tired after hours of walking, she found a narrow road which wound down to Winsford and settled by a crystal stream to enjoy a cream tea. She made a little ritual out of slicing the light scones, heaping them with cream and glistening homemade strawberry jam.

Where should she go next? She planned it all. A week in Malta?

In the past she'd preferred holiday destinations where the swimming was

The wild ponies' moulting russet hair would be seized on by nesting birds

and new growth where honey-scented primroses presented a modest sweetness. Above her, the keen deep blue of an April sky was coaxing the chilled earth slowly towards summer.

She passed knotted beech roots, worn bare by rain and the activities of rabbits, which laced the hedges and then lost

good, and the family had been to Malta several times. The flying distance was only four hours, the water warm and clear.

The children had loved to swim too, and now she was alone she visited all the old places and recollected Mark's first major dive off that particular rock or

Continued overleaf

Sophie's triumph the first time she'd swum across the Blue Lagoon.

Now she reconnected with the scents of hot limestone, the sea and the thyme which bristled among the rocks. She made pets of the lizards which darted out of their crevices and flicked long tongues at the juices of melon and tomato which she pushed towards them. She gave herself up to the turquoise depths with languorous strokes, hovering above a little family of fish which nuzzled the rocks and which allowed her within a couple of feet of them before flashing away.

In a balmy dusk, she visited the village

She filled her senses with the glories of the earth. And thus she filled many months

of Nadur on Gozo at festa time and listened to the voices of children singing on the steps of the huge, domed church.

Later, she drove to the west coast of Scotland to walk on the white sands of deserted beaches, and climbed the hills in gentle mists to listen to perfect silence. The sky, the sea and the hills gave her a sense of peace, for they are eternal things, bringing into proportion the transient struggles and trials of man.

Each day brought her greater riches. She filled her senses with the manifold glories of the earth, of life itself. Thus she filled many months.

The debriefing was over. Now she had to face the media.

"And how did you survive the solitary incarceration in a cell eight feet by ten feet for so long?" The journalists bristled with cameras and that strange, questing energy they carried about with them.

"My captors treated me well." And they had, as best they could. They had even expressed their regret when they'd discovered their mistake.

"Claustrophobia? No books? No news? No contact of any kind?" Surely anyone would suffer mental anguish? They wanted their story. She was a journalist herself. She understood.

Smiling, she said, "To imprison the body is one thing. Quite another to imprison the mind. Memories and imagination are wonderful things."

. . . .

THE AUTHOR SAYS...

"I sometimes wonder how much of our lives we live in our imagination. I have to admit to a great deal!"

Brain BOOSTERS

Codeword

Each letter of the alphabet has been replaced by a number. The numbers for the first name of our pictured celebrity are given. Colin Firth first rose to prominence as Mr Darcy in *Pride and Prejudice*, but in which other film did he also portray a character named Mr Darcy?

| A | B | C̶ | D | E | F | G | H | I̶ | J | K | L̶ | M | N̶ | O̶ | P | Q | R | S | T | U | V | W | X | Y | Z |

1	2	3 N	4	5	6	7 C	8	9	10	11 I	12	13
14	15	16 L	17	18	19 O	20	21	22	23	24	25	26

| 2 | 1 | 12 I | 6 | 21 | 11 | 26 | | 24 | 19 | 3 O | N | 11 | 20 | | 20 | | 6 | 12 I | 23 | 1 | 8 |

A Holiday Romance?

Absolutely not! All I wanted was to find my own feet, beside lovely Lake Garda

By Linda Lewis

I t's been five years, Barbara. You can't stay at home for ever. Why don't you go on one of those singles holidays at Easter? See the sights."

My sister gave me a hug. "It's time you had some fun. You never know, you might meet someone. A holiday romance would do you the world of good."

At the words "holiday romance", I struggled out of her embrace.

"No, thank you very much. I'm too old for that kind of nonsense. Besides, everyone knows they never amount to anything."

Anita gave me one of her looks.

"You're only fifty three, Barbara. Anyway, who says holiday romances don't work out? Some of them must." She lowered her voice. "I wish I could come on holiday with you. Going to Spain so that Bill can play endless rounds of golf isn't a lot of fun."

That made me laugh out loud.

"Really? You'd go to the North Pole

Continued overleaf

ILLUSTRATIONS: REX/SHUTTERSTOCK, MANDY DIXON

Continued from previous page
and stay in an igloo if Bill wanted to."

Anita pretended to think about it, then grinned ruefully.

"I would too," she said, her eyes taking on the dreamy look they always had when she thought of her husband.

I felt a prickle of envy. After thirty-six years together, she was still as potty about him as the day they were married. Happily for her, he was every bit as potty about her, too.

That night, I couldn't sleep for thinking about what Anita had said.

Since I lost Phil, I'd hardly gone anywhere. I spent my days off mooching about, or catching up on my reading.

I wasn't looking for anyone else… but that didn't mean I couldn't go on holiday.

I'd wanted to go to Italy for years but

As I settled into my seat on the plane, my hands shook as I did up the seat belt. Then the engines started to roar as we raced down the runway…

"Are you OK?" the man sitting next to me asked in concern. "Only you're clenching your fists so tightly, your knuckles have gone white."

They had, too.

"I'm a bit nervous," I admitted. "I've never flown before."

He nodded. "That's understandable then – but statistically, flying is by far the safest way to travel."

"I know. I'm not actually scared, more apprehensive about this whole holiday thing," I said, suddenly feeling like confiding in him. "I lost my husband five years ago, you see – this is actually the first time I've been away on my own."

"I'm sorry," he said. After a while, he

"I'm sure they wouldn't mind if you joined us. Dining by yourself, that's always hard…"

Phil wasn't keen. Most of the time we went for breaks to Cornwall or the Lake District. He said he preferred to stay in England – but I knew the truth was that he hated the thought of flying and was such a bad sailor, even the ferry to the Isle of Wight made him feel queasy.

I didn't mind. I was happy as long as we were together. Still, now I was on my own I could go where I liked.

A couple of days later, I found the perfect holiday in Italy. The hotel was on the shores of Lake Garda.

There were various excursions too, but I didn't book any of those. The plan was to enjoy exploring on my own.

spoke again. "So – two firsts in one. That's really brave." He held out his hand. "I'm Ian. Ian Fletcher."

"Barbara White. Pleased to meet you." We started chatting and in what felt like no time at all, the flight was over. The crew announced that we would soon be coming in to land.

"Where are you staying?" Ian asked as he did up his seat belt.

I named the hotel. "Apparently, it's right on the shores of Lake Garda."'

"That's great." His smile lit up his face. "I'm staying there too."

"Really?"

He nodded towards the other side of

the plane. "I'm with a group but I'm sure they wouldn't mind if you joined us. Even if it's just for meals. Dining by yourself, that's always hard."

I said I'd think about it, but that was a fib. I'd already decided to go it alone. As the plane descended, I glanced at Ian. Like an excited child, his nose was practically glued to the porthole.

We'd got on so well, and had so much in common, I was tempted to say yes, I'd join his group, but the idea of the holiday was to relax and get used to exploring by myself. Ian seemed very nice – but as I'd told my sister in no uncertain terms, this holiday wasn't about finding love, it was about finding my feet again after losing my husband.

At least, that was the plan… but my resolve didn't last long.

Even as I ate my first meal at a table in the corner laid for one, the noise and the laughter drifting across from Ian's group kept drawing my gaze. He must have noticed me looking because he soon came over and asked if I'd like to sit with them. In the end it seemed churlish not to, especially when there was an empty place, right next to Ian.

As I sat down, the woman at the head of the table, who I guessed was in charge of the group, called out a welcome and said I could join them on their various trips.

"We're not full," she said. "Besides, there's always room for a small one."

"See," said Ian. "I told you we were a friendly bunch."

By the end of the meal, I'd caved in.

The next seven days were idyllic. Italy was as glorious as I'd imagined. Even in the smallest village, every corner revealed a view that begged to be photographed.

Thanks to my digital camera, I could keep snapping away to my heart's content. I even ventured up the funicular railway to spectacular Monte Baldo and took some great shots of other groups paragliding from the summit – that was a little too adventurous for us to try!

Yet it wasn't just the scenery, the food and the endless ice cream that I loved; it felt good being part of a group, and if I'm honest, I liked having Ian by my side. He'd lost his wife three years ago so he understood what I'd been through but it was more than that. It might be a cliché, but we just seemed to click.

On the last night of the holiday, he suggested a stroll by the lake. As we wandered down to the water's edge, the sun was about to set. I hardly knew where to look, it was all so stunningly beautiful; the sky, a riot of pinks and red and yellows, the church silhouetted against the mountains, the inky stillness of the water. It was breathtaking.

Continued overleaf

I closed my eyes and let out a long sigh. Unfortunately, Ian chose that moment to take me in his arms and try to kiss me.

I was so surprised, I stiffened and jumped away as though I'd been stung.

"I'm sorry," he said. "I've obviously crossed a line."

I didn't know what to say. I could have explained, admitted I'd been hoping he might kiss me for days – but what was the point? It would just be a holiday romance. Everyone knows what happens to those.

We walked back, hardly saying a word, the inches between us feeling like yards.

At the hotel, he wished me goodnight.

"So, this is goodbye. I don't expect I'll see you in the morning. Your flight's much earlier than ours."

Then he asked for my phone number.

I shook my head.

"I'm not sure that's a good idea," I said then I dashed to the safety of my room before he could try to change my mind.

I couldn't stop thinking about him on the flight home, wondering if I'd made a mistake – we'd got along so well. But if there was one thing I didn't want, it was a broken heart.

My sister met me at the airport.

"Welcome home," she called eagerly. "How was Italy? Did you have a good time? Did you meet anyone?"

She threw questions at me so fast, I held up a hand in surrender.

"I'll tell you all about it when we get home. Right now, I'm dying for a decent cup of tea."

Once we were home, over several cups of tea, I told her all about my trip – everything except Ian, that is.

When I eventually paused for breath, Anita gave my arm an enthusiastic nudge.

"And?"

"It was wonderful," I breathed. "Perfect weather. Perfect hotel. The food, the walking, the views. It was all amazing. Wait until you see the photos."

Anita smiled. "Come on, sis. There's something you're not telling me." She paused, her blue eyes twinkling. "This group you teamed up with. You met somebody, didn't you?"

I blushed. "OK. I admit it." I told her a bit about Ian, "but don't get excited. I'm not planning on seeing him again."

She raised her left eyebrow.

"So you're just going to let this lovely man walk out of your life – a kind, good-looking widower with soft brown eyes, who lives less than twenty miles away."

I shrugged. "You know what they say about holiday romances. It's all about being somewhere different, away from your everyday life. It's not real. Remember that time in Whitby? I met that boy who promised to keep in touch."

"What? Good grief." She laughed. "That was nearly forty years ago! Besides, what 'they' say, whoever they are, is that they *often* end in tears. That doesn't mean they *always* do." She gave me her

over the friend request button trying to summon up the courage to press it, when my boss materialised behind my shoulder, like a ghost.

I spun round and started to apologise but she cut me off mid-sentence.

"Never mind all that," she said. "There's a dishy man in reception, asking to see you. He says it's important."

As I stepped out of the lift, his back was towards me but I would have

When his face appeared on the screen, my heart lurched – and my boss appeared

best, most piercing stare. "You like this man, don't you? I can see it written all over your face."

"Yes," I admitted, "but…"

She didn't let me finish.

"Then call him."

"I can't. I don't have his number."

"Does he have yours?"

"No. He asked for it, but I said no."

"*Really*, Barbara." Anita let out an exasperated sigh. "You're hopeless. Never mind, you should be able to find him easily enough – after all, everyone's on Facebook these days."

She pulled out her smart phone.

"Let me get unpacked first," I joked.

"Fine." She made me promise to look for him when I went back to work the following Monday.

Spending time on Facebook was strictly against the rules, but that wasn't the only reason I felt nervous as I logged on. It didn't take long to find Ian.

When his face appeared on the screen, my heart lurched. My finger was hovering

recognised him from any angle. My heart, already racing, began doing the quickstep.

"Ian? Is that you?"

He turned with a tentative smile.

"You said where you worked, so –" He shrugged. "The thing is, Barbara –"

I tried to interrupt, but he held up a hand. "Please. Don't say anything or I'll lose my nerve." He took a deep breath. "I've grown very fond of you over the past week. You made it clear that you don't want a romantic relationship and that's OK with me. But the thing is, I'd really like to see you again – even if only as friends."

I didn't say a word, I simply put my arms around his neck and held him.

That was four months ago. It turns out that my sister was right about holiday romances. Just sometimes, everything works out fine.

THE AUTHOR SAYS...

"It took me many years to find the courage to go abroad on my own. Sadly, I didn't find love!"

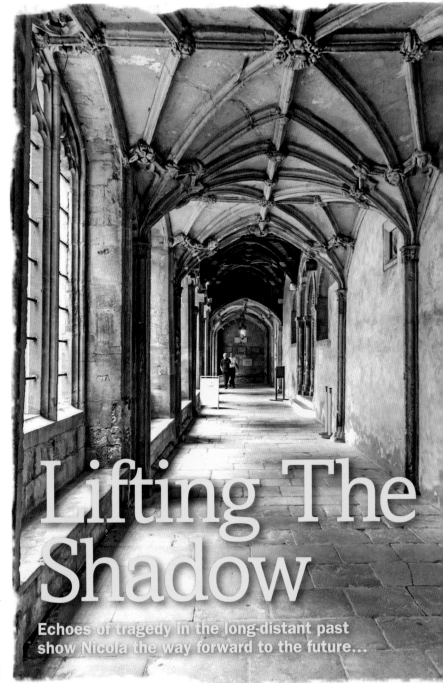

Lifting The Shadow

Echoes of tragedy in the long-distant past show Nicola the way forward to the future...

By Valerie Bowes

The sigh breathed over the empty trenches of the excavation. Nicola looked up from her meticulous drawing and rubbed the goosebumps that had erupted on her bare arms. It was the wind, that's all it was – but it had sounded unnervingly like a sigh, and she could feel a sadness clinging to her like mist.

Maybe she just needed a break, like the others. She paused, torn between her desire to finish her recording of the stones and the siren call of the tea-room.

The tea-room won.

Lingering unease was dispelled as she shoved open the door that separated the twenty-first century from the fourteenth, and heard the familiar sound of Steve Brunyard and Patsy Wells arguing.

"It's only a legend, Steve. Someone sees a shadow, thinks 'ghostly nun' and bingo! You've got her walled up before you can say *Sound of Music*."

"It's a pretty persistent legend, though. There've been stories about it going back to the Dissolution."

"Well, there you go!" Patsy threw her hands wide with the air of someone who has proved their point. "Nothing like a nice bit of adverse publicity if you're going to suppress the monasteries, right?"

"What she do to get walled up?" asked one of the diggers.

"Got herself pregnant. Big no-no if you're a nun, that – even if most of them had just been shoved into a convent by their families. She was supposed to have indulged in a spot of rumpy with the chap in the church – Sir Somebody de Bruiniard – late fourteenth century or thereabouts.

Continued overleaf

He has quite a nice effigy, with his feet propped up on a little dog – although he wouldn't have been a Crusader, not at that date. Maybe he was just fond of dogs." Patsy dug her elbow teasingly in Steve's ribs. "Relative of yours, Stevie?"

"I like dogs." Steve shook his head. "But I'm not into nuns."

Are you into crimson hair and silver nose-rings, then? Nicola thought, with a glance at Patsy. The sharpness of the sting of jealousy surprised and puzzled her. Steve was tall and broad-shouldered, with dark hair and nice eyes, but she wasn't attracted to him… was she? His glance met hers for a moment. She smiled uncertainly – and he smiled back.

"Well, I think it would be rather fun to find out," Patsy said. "Stranger things have happened. That bloke in Cheddar has the same DNA as one of the Stone Age skeletons they found in the cave."

there for eight hundred years, so I don't suppose they're going anywhere for ten minutes." She almost told him about the sigh, but the sorrow was too real somehow. It was best keep it to herself, or everyone would think she was going doolally. "You reckon we're going to get everything out before the deadline?"

He grimaced. "I hope so, or the developers will start getting stroppy. Like the world really needs another shopping mall! Can't they see that once this is gone, it's gone – and all that history and knowledge with it?"

Once the break was over and the trenches were full of people beavering away, Nicola found it was easy to convince herself that she'd merely imagined the feeling of desolation. She finished recording the bared foundations of the cloister and turned her attention to the next section of trench.

"Patsy's got some lovely wall in hers,

The feeling of despair that seeped from the unearthed cavity was too deep to ignore

"Fancy me in armour, would you?"

Steve put on a pantomime leer and Patsy slapped his hand away.

"In your dreams! Anyway, I reckon the carving was done later, because the style of helmet definitely looks suss for that period."

"No way!" Round the table, heads were nodded or shaken vehemently.

The others joined enthusiastically in the debate, but Steve got up and came to sit by Nicola as she sipped her tea.

"Finished?" he asked.

"Not quite, but those stones have been

the jammy cow," one digger said. "There's nothing in this but some natural… might as well close it down."

"It's one more piece for the jigsaw," Nicola consoled him. "At least we know we must be outside the walls from here."

By the next morning, Patsy had exposed enough of the length of wall for Nicola to begin recording. She crouched on her stool, transferring the stone reality to lines on paper, oblivious to the bee-hive busy-ness around her. A bell struck its silvery notes in her ear and she

hunched a shoulder irritably… *don't be daft. It can't be Vespers yet.*

Shade moved across her drawing.

"Come on, Patsy! Get out of the light, will you?"

The usual rude reply didn't come and Nicola looked up. Patsy was at the other end of the trench, and at the back of Nicola's mind, she knew the regular scrape of the trowel hadn't ceased. She frowned and glanced down at the paper, gleaming white and shadow-free.

"Oi, Patsy," she called out. "What's with the bell?"

"You what?" Patsy said, without looking up.

"The bell."

"What bell?"

"Never mind." Nicola suddenly didn't want to talk about it.

Why had she so automatically assumed that the bell signified one of the Masses that punctuated the convent day? How would she know – she wasn't a specialist in medieval monastic Houses; she wouldn't be able to tell her Vespers from her Matins.

Get a grip, girl, she told herself severely. *You poke about among the detritus of the dead for a living, and you've been in spookier places than this. Why start imagining things now?*

She heard no more sighs or silver chimes and saw no more unexplained shadows, but she couldn't shake off the growing feeling that *something* was about to happen.

"Hey, Nic, come and see this!" Patsy's voice penetrated her concentration. "I can get my trowel right in here. There's a space behind and it looks like something's been blocked up. Give us a hand to shift that masonry – it might be a door."

Nicola put down her drawing and went to stare at the patch of stonework.

"It's a cavity," she said.

Patsy shrugged. "Could be… what makes you think so?"

I just know. "Is it worth messing about with? It's all going to be demolished in a couple of weeks when they start building." Her words went against every archaeological creed, but the despair that seeped from the crack was too deep to be ignored. She didn't want to see what lay behind the stone.

Patsy formed her two index fingers into a cross and held them up at her. "You go and wash your mouth out, Nicola Lamm! That's sacrilege! You'd never have got on *Time Team* by saying things like that!" She beckoned over Nicola's shoulder. "Steve, come and give us a hand. Nic's gone all work-shy."

Diggers began to drift towards the trench, drawn by the sixth sense that set jungle drums tapping whenever a decent find was about to be made. Nicola watched, mesmerised, as Steve and Patsy

Continued overleaf

extracted chunks of stone, like dentists pulling teeth.

"There's something here," Patsy called. "It's a burial, I think." She picked delicately at a scrap of material that had once been black, now so fragile it could have been a desiccated leaf.

"Let's have a look." Steve peered down. "Wait a minute. This skeleton hasn't been laid out, it's collapsed in on itself. And the cavity's tiny." His voice betrayed his excitement. "It's not a burial, it's an immuration. So the legend was true!"

"The bit about someone getting walled up is true," corrected the practical Patsy. "The rest of it could be a load of old cobblers. Can you see if there's any sign of an infant?"

"Doesn't look like it," Steve said.

She saved the baby. Thank God, Alyson saved the baby.

"There could be a foetus in there somewhere, but I'm not a bone expert. We'll have

to get hold of Francesca." Steve pushed himself up from his knees coming level with Nicola. He grinned at her. "What about that, eh? Proves we should pay more attention to folk tales."

The pathetic little heap of bones filled Nicola with an inexplicable anguish. The girl had been so small, so defenceless. Had she and the knight who lay in the church truly loved each other, or had he merely satisfied the lust of a moment on her? It had been his child – or so the story went.

"You OK, Nic?" Steve's voice reached her from a long way away, as she stood pinned in her place by a melancholy that made her feel as if she'd been doused in icy water. "You've gone an awfully funny colour, Nic."

He reached out in concern, but she backed away.

"I feel sick," she managed, and fled to the sanctuary of the toilets.

The face that looked back at her from the mirror as she washed her hands was as white as a wimple.

Wishing she could say one of the prayers that the nun would have known, a picture of the tiny Norman church down the road rose in Nicola's mind.

She'd been meaning to go and see it while she was here. It was as good a place as any to say a prayer… any prayer.

Somewhat ashamed of her intention, she slipped away from the excavation and walked the few hundred yards to where the church squatted under its square tower.

The latch clunked when she tried the huge twisted metal ring and the door responded to her push. A woman arranging flowers by the altar gave Nicola a welcoming smile.

"Do come in. I'm just about finished here, but stay as long as you like. I'll be over in the Hall for another half hour or so at least, if you need me."

"It's alright, thanks. I only want to have a quick look round."

"There's guidebooks in the cupboard there – they're £1.50. It all goes towards the upkeep. Can you let me know when you leave, so I can come and lock up?"

"Sure," Nicola said.

The woman nodded a smiling goodbye and Nicola chinked coins into the box.

The knight was lying on his low, bed-like tomb, palms pressed prayerfully together, blank eyes staring into the distance of piety. His bearded face was bland and anonymous under the conical helmet and Nicola remembered Patsy's theory about the carving being later. She flipped the pages of the booklet.

T*he fine fourteenth-century effigy is that of Sir Stephen de Bruiniard (1351 – 1384?) killed on campaign in Scotland. He is reputed, in local legend, to have seduced a nun of Mountsfield Priory and fathered a child on her. The unfortunate Nichole Pavin, known as Sister Agnes, is popularly supposed to have been walled up in the convent with her baby.*

Nicola shivered and dropped the booklet, pressing the heels of her hands so hard against her eyes that when she

"God's greeting, Nichole."

The world steadied a little, still poised on the point of a pin, but the words came from then, not now... didn't they?

She must have misheard, been working too hard, that was all. It put added stress on everyone when you were digging with an army of JCBs practically crawling up your back.

She made a supreme effort of will and focussed on the man who now stood in the nave.

"Steve – you made me jump!" she said, tempering her accusation with a smile. "Did you come to check up on the legend? Look, it's in the booklet."

She picked it up and held it out, but he remained rigid, his eyes as blank and unmoving as the effigy's. A stab of fear stole her breath for a moment, before anger replaced it.

"What's up with you?" she demanded crisply. "Here, have a look if you want to." She thrust the booklet at him, but he took

Shadows closed in on her, memories flashing like disconnected dreams

removed them, she could see nothing but red flashing lights in front of her.

Suddenly, she heard the door open.

A man's footsteps came down the short aisle, brisk at first, slowing to a stumbling stop. Giddiness made her head swim.

The past and the present teetered like a see-saw... faces and names tumbled through her brain... Alyson the midwife and Lady Johanna de Bruiniard, Prioress Katrine, implacable with conviction... Patsy with the crimson hair...

Steve.

both it and her hand in a crushing grip.

"Betrayed," he sighed heavily on a downward breath.

"I did not! It was your wife!"

For a moment, Nicola didn't realise what she'd said, then her heart began to pound in long, slow thumps. Shadows seemed to close in on her, memories flashing like disconnected dreams. Pain and flickering candles in a hut smelling of goats; the cry of a baby; the discomfort of the ox-cart in the chill grey light... the

Continued overleaf

Continued from previous page

sound of a trowel on stone… a woman whose face beneath the conical head-dress was full of triumphant spite.

"Not you. Never you," the strange man said hoarsely. "Mine was the fault." His hand tightened and she cried out.

"You hurt me!"

"The horses were ready, but you never came. I waited until I could wait no longer. The King had summoned me. I had to go."

She clawed at fingers that were as unyielding as stone. "I could not come. I was bearing your child! Stephen, loose me. It is time for forgiveness."

we can give her the proper burial that was denied her – and leave them at peace, together."

A deep breath seemed to fill the little church for a moment. Warmth seeped back into Steve's eyes and his softening fingers.

"Nic? So will you?"

"Will I what?" She blinked at him, bewildered.

He shook his head slightly, a puzzled frown followed by a rueful smile.

"I don't know… you spend weeks trying to screw up enough courage to ask someone to have dinner with you and, when you finally do, she's more interested

She clawed at fingers that were as unyielding as stone as they gripped hers

"I cannot forgive myself."

From somewhere deep within Nicola, gladness rose in a flood… he *had* loved her. He had not been a party to his wife's betrayal. The Lady Johanna had lied in order to wound.

It did not matter now who had told his wife where to find Sir Stephen's mistress, or why – jealousy, religious conviction, or hope of reward – for it made no difference now.

The darkness ebbed, the past spiralled back into the past, and Nicola knew she stood in the little Norman church beside a centuries-old tomb.

"Steve, listen to me. I'm not Nichole Pavin, and you're not Sir Stephen."

She spoke loudly and insistently, desperate to reach past those unnervingly unseeing eyes.

"No matter what happened back then, what's done is done. We can't alter it, but

in some guy who lived over six hundred years ago."

The warmth spread, wrapping Nicola in contentment.

"Well, I reckon Patsy's right." Her happiness was making her light-headed. "This effigy was done later. The helmet's definitely suss."

She tucked her hand in Steve's and laid her cheek against his arm, looking fondly down at the bearded face which seemed to tell her not to waste this God-given second chance.

The shadows of the past had lifted and they had no more power.

● ●

THE AUTHOR SAYS…

"I've always been interested in history and once did an evening class on archaeology, which was fascinating. Perhaps one day I'll get to go on a dig."

Double Choc Chip & Cherry Muffins

Mmm – these delicious muffins are simply yummy!

Ingredients (Serves 8)

- ✦ **200g plain flour**
- ✦ **2tsp baking powder**
- ✦ **Pinch of salt**
- ✦ **100g caster sugar**
- ✦ **50g dark chocolate, chopped**
- ✦ **50g white chocolate, chopped**
- ✦ **100g glace cherries, quartered**
- ✦ **50g butter, melted**
- ✦ **1 large egg**
- ✦ **1tsp vanilla extract**
- ✦ **100ml milk**

1 Preheat the oven to 200°C, fan oven 180°C, Gas Mark 6. Place 8 paper muffin cases into a muffin tray, or you can line with squares of greaseproof paper.

2 Sift the flour and baking powder into a mixing bowl, then stir in the sugar, chopped chocolate and glace cherries.

3 In a jug, beat together the cooled melted butter, egg, vanilla and milk. Add to the dry ingredients and stir until just combined. Do not over-mix.

4 Spoon the mixture into the paper cases and bake for 20-25 minutes until risen and golden. Cool on a wire rack before serving.

Cook's tip: For truly successful muffins avoid over-mixing the dry and wet ingredients.

RECIPES AND FOOD STYLING: SUE ASHWORTH PICTURES: JONATHAN SHORT

Summer Holiday

Feel the sand under your feet, taste the ice cream and revel in the wistful nostalgia of long-lost true love…

By Ellie Edwards

H ello? Can you help us? We just found this in the sand."
Two little faces peered up over the sill of my ice cream van.

A small, hot hand thrust towards me, brandishing a key with a small silver fish attached. I took it gently and leaned forward to get a better look at my visitors.

The taller of the two, a girl, bore the expression of a long-suffering mother despite being all of nine years old. The smaller child – a boy – was about six and had a bright, cheeky face dusted with freckles and sand.

"I found it!" he grinned. "In the dunes. I saw it in the sand, like a real fish. Margo told me we had to hand it in because someone might be looking for it. Margo's my sister."

"Freddy wanted to keep it. I explained it wasn't right to do that," she informed me, in an endearingly grown-up tone.

"Hmmm, let's see… Yes, Freddy, it's true, this looks like a hotel key and could be extremely important. Imagine if a person is here on the beach, in nothing but swimming trunks and goes to get changed for dinner but he can't get into his room!"

Freddy's face turned into a cartoon expression of delight at the image.

"He'd have to go to the restaurant in bare feet and trunks!" he gasped.

"He could ask the receptionist to let him in to his room," ventured Margo, very reasonably. "They do that, you know. I've seen it on films."

"Quite right. Well, I think you've both been very sensible in bringing this key to my ice cream van. You both deserve a congratulatory ice cream for your honesty and good citizenship."

As they sauntered happily back up the beach slurping their rewards, I took a closer look at the keyring.

The silver fish was the length of a finger, pleasantly smooth and rounded. On the back, "Seafoam" had been inscribed, suggesting to me an establishment that had named its rooms rather than attributing numbers.

There was nothing else, but I figured that I could do some detective work online to find the right hotel.

The rest of the afternoon passed quickly as the clouds dispersed and the crowds thickened. I've known this resort for forty years and it still pulls at my heart-

Continued overleaf

The children sauntered happily back along
the beach, slurping their rewards

Continued from previous page

strings to see the beach in full swing. Families stumble down the path clutching bags, towels and babies, hesitating before they select their prime spot. Teenagers tumble over the dunes, landing in heaps and carelessly throwing down towels.

Occasionally, there are children like Margo and Freddy who have been sent "to get some fresh air" and of course, you have the older couples who set up camps of comfy deckchairs and cool-boxes, then stroll along the shore, hand in hand. Those are the ones who make my heart sigh.

At fifty-six, I envy the slow contentment of older sweethearts far more than the teens with their energy and optimism. I've had my fair share of youthful exuberance and some of the best days of my life were spent right on this very beach. Truth be told, it's why I'm still here, forty years after my first summer.

Holidays were far simpler back in the seventies. Programmes like *Wish You Were Here* with Judith Chalmers were new and aspirational, revealing exotic places like Benidorm, but most viewers never dreamed of hopping on a plane for two weeks in foreign sunshine.

Our family would travel to Bournemouth and I'd be squashed between my brother and sister. Dad was a carpet-fitter and, near the end of every August, he'd strip out the van then bolt in the bench seat. We'd sit in a line, over-excited and impatient, competing to catch our first glimpse of the sea. If we were lucky, Dad would put on his eight-track tapes of The Beatles or The Who and Mum would hand out bottles of Panda pop.

I'll never forget the summer that Celia's tummy took a dislike to cherry fizz, but that's a story for another time!

The first time we came here, I would have been just sixteen. Tall for my age, my dad was forever reminding me to stand up straight, especially that summer.

Looking back, I probably looked like most other teenagers but at the time I remember feeling conspicuous and ungainly, hair sprouting where it hadn't before and an attraction to the opposite sex that made me suddenly shy of getting changed on a beach.

I remember as vividly as if it were yesterday the first time I saw Caterina standing at the shore. Our family had set up base in the usual spot, strategically between the steps, sea and refreshment booth. I'd started walking towards the water when this vision of a young woman in nothing but a costume stopped me in my tracks. I felt my face burn with a mixture of desire, shame and confusion. She was beautiful by anyone's standards but she simply stood, gazing at the horizon as if unaware of anything or anyone around her. I, on the other hand, felt utterly exposed yet I couldn't take my eyes off her.

"Ethan! What are you gawping at?"

My sister, Celia, barged into me on her route to the waves, knocking me off balance so that I almost fell. Her laughter prompted the young woman to turn and look at me and in that very moment, when those dark, almond eyes met mine, I knew. It was as if a little voice in my head murmured, "Of course."

If I had more money, I could have treated her to something. I only had a pound note

Almost immediately after, my little brother Mikey bashed my knee with his bucket as he ran past, and the spell was broken – but not before I'd gained a slow smile from her.

I'd love to tell you that we spent lazy days and lingering evenings in each other's arms, and that it was a summer love that eased into a lifetime, but it wasn't so simple. In fact, that first summer, the only time I spoke to her was the next day at the refreshment booth.

"Oh, sorry, were you were before me?" she asked. I had been, but gestured her to go ahead.

"So, umm," I muttered, desperate not to let the opportunity go. "You here with your family, too?"

"Um-hmm, we come to my aunt's every summer. I love this beach."

"Me, too." My brain tried to think of something irresistibly seductive but failed. We shuffled forward in the queue. I didn't have much time. If I'd had more money I could have treated her to something, but I only had a pound note.

"My name's Ethan," I blurted, and her face broke into a symphony of a smile. Angels might have sung, at that point.

"Well, hello, Ethan – I'm Caterina." This sounded wonderfully exotic. All the girls in my school were called Sharon, Stephanie or Tracy.

"Oh! Here we go, ice cream time. I love ice cream, don't you?"

I did; I still do. I love how ice cream can make us all children again.

I'm an ice cream man today because of her, really – not because of my

Continued overleaf

excellent education and track record managing blue-chip companies. A stress-related heart-attack at fifty-two stopped me short and when I was strongly advised to opt for a relaxed lifestyle, my first thought, out of the blue, was selling ice creams on Bournemouth beach.

Of course all my colleagues thought I was joking. Even my former boss asked me gently, with the best intentions, if I was quite sure what I was doing. The truth was, despite various relationships through the years, I'd never completely forgotten my first love, Caterina – and while I'd excelled working in the city, part of me had always remained here, because my adoration of Caterina lasted way beyond that first conversation.

We bumped into each other the following summer, when she surpassed even the dreams I'd conjured of her eyes, smile and figure over the intervening months. Of course, all the

that I'd already placed Caterina on a pedestal, aided by the fact that I had seen her in a bikini on several occasions. She was a lot to live up to.

Yet, in that summer of 1977, when we finally became boyfriend and girlfriend, Caterina lived up to everything; I was utterly smitten, became the best version of myself when I was with her – and the worst sort of moping puppy when I wasn't.

"Ethan, for heaven's sakes, we've hardly seen you at all," Mum complained, plastering Mikey with suncream. "The reason I persuaded your Dad to come for three weeks this time was to really enjoy our time as a family before you go off to university. Instead, you wolf down your breakfast, grab a sandwich and you're out all day with this girl!"

"But Mum…"

"Ethan, I understand that you've got feelings for her, I do remember what it's like, but listen to what I'm saying. We've only got five days left. Once we get home, it's a couple of weeks and you'll be off."

I knew what Mum was saying and she

"It's the end of summer. We leave on Friday," Margo said. Freddy deflated visibly

elegant phrases I'd composed disappeared from my mind when I saw her, so that we only had a few very ordinary conversations. It wasn't until the third summer that we finally became close.

What can I tell you that you won't already know about teenage romances? I was eighteen by then, and although I'd had a few girlfriends at school, I was no Casanova. My sentimental nature meant

was right. Uni was only weeks away, but I was desperate to see Caterina at every available moment. All those pop songs about feeling sick when you're not with the one you love had made sense this summer. It was dreadful… but the pay-off was wonderful.

Of that summer with Caterina I have nothing but wonderful memories. Looking back, Mum was right about that being our last holiday as a family: we sat around the little caravan every evening playing card games and eating shortbread, or cooking bacon and eggs on the gas stove.

They are some of my happiest, most precious memories. Dad passed away a few years ago and only then did I realise how little I'd seen him after I'd left home.

It's encouraged me to spend more time visiting Mum, occasionally bringing her to stay in the spare room of my seaview apartment. She loves to stroll along the seafront here as well, reminiscing.

As for Celia and Mike, we all catch up now and again but their lives are as busy as mine always was, before I fled to the sea. Celia has written this off as a midlife crisis, and Mike – a marine biologist – celebrates the craziness of his white-collar older brother becoming a sandal-wearing ice-cream vendor.

The kids, Margo and Freddy, returned the following day to ask if the owner of the key had materialised.

"No, but I think the key is from a hotel at the other end of the seafront," I confided. "I left them a message this

morning, so maybe we'll solve this mystery before you guys go home. How long are you here?"

"It's the end of summer. We leave on Friday," said Margo. Freddy deflated visibly at the thought.

"It's not fair. I want to stay on holiday for always," he pouted, and I rather agreed with him.

After our magical fortnight together, Caterina and I stayed in touch, reuniting for a second glorious holiday then writing letters and calling, but eventually, we drifted apart. We lived too far from each other to maintain the romance and it was tougher back then, pre-internet.

Years later, I tried searching for her online but it never came to anything. The one link I had, her father's restaurant business, had been bought out and the family had moved on.

I had a couple of long-term relationships but mostly I focused on my career. Fat lot of good that did me. No, that's not true; I have a fantastic apartment and enough investments to ensure that the ice cream van can be purely for pleasure and company.

Yet my sentimental heart had never quite been satisfied.

Of course, you've probably already guessed why this story had to be told. That evening, when I answered the phone, it took my breath away.

"Hello, I'm sorry I couldn't do so earlier, but I'm returning your call about the key ring."

"That's right, I –"

"Sorry to interrupt, but, in your

Continued overleaf

Continued from previous page

message, did you say Ethan Varney?"

Suddenly I recognised her voice.

Yes, it's crazy and ludicrous and wonderful. The local paper did a colour feature and some TV people got in touch asking to film at the wedding – it's unbelievable!

until now. Having met for the first time at summer's end, it didn't surprise me in the least that we would finally be together at the summer's end of our lives.

"Don't you feel sad for the time you missed?" asked one interviewer.

"Not at all!" laughed Caterina. "We feel happy for the lives we've had, and

It's obvious that we were meant to be together... but obviously not until now

The very next morning when Caterina's figure approached the ice cream van, my heart lifted, then dipped, then soared. I got out and we just stood there, looking at each other. We've both been through decades of living, but in that moment all that mattered was that we were both there again, on our beach.

"Ethan," she whispered, and put her hand to my face, exactly as I remembered.

"I tried to find you, Caterina, but I couldn't. Did you… change your name?"

"I never married," she said, answering the implied question, then blushed. "Caterina is my middle name, from my Italian mother. My first name is Stephanie, that's why you never found me. For you I wanted to be Caterina, not to be ordinary."

As if anyone could be more extraordinary.

Over lunch, we discovered we'd both moved back to the same beach within a month of each other – me to my apartment and ice cream van, Caterina to open a boutique hotel. We were obviously meant to be together, but obviously not

immensely thankful that we found each other again. Nothing to regret."

That's the headline they chose for the newspaper article. Best of all, the paper paid for Freddy and Margot to come back to Bournemouth and presented them with a Good Citizenship award.

Caterina and I have offered them free ice creams for life and a week's holiday at the hotel every year, but frankly they seem most pleased about the ice creams for now.

Of course it defies the odds that the key should have been handed to me, of all people, and that we should have found each after so long – but that's what love does, isn't it? It defies the odds.

We're both older, but we're together and life's very sunny.

This year, as the season ends, it feels as if my summer is only just beginning.

• •

THE AUTHOR SAYS...

"Having once found a key on a beach, it set me thinking about where I should hand it in and, of course, what the story might be behind it."

FANCY THAT!

Fascinating facts about **outer space**

✦ Hypervelocity Stars are luminous balls of gas that hurtle through space at trillions of miles per hour.

✦ **Space officially begins at the invisible Karman Line, 100km above the Earth. If you could drive your car straight up, you'd be in space in less than an hour.**

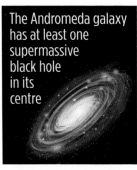

The Andromeda galaxy has at least one supermassive black hole in its centre

✦ If you piled up all visible matter in the universe it would be only 5% of the total mass. 27% is "dark matter" and the rest is "dark energy" that is pushing the universe apart at high speed.

✦ **Neptune has the fastest wind speeds in our solar system at a staggering 1600mph!**

Sagittarius B12 is ethyl formate, the gas that gives raspberries their taste and rum its smell – if you wondered what the centre of our galaxy smells and tastes like...

✦ Cancri 55 is an entire planet made of diamond – and it's 4 times bigger than Earth!

✦ **More energy from the Sun hits Earth every hour than the entire** planet uses in a whole year. Get those solar panels up and running...

✦ Voyager 1, launched in 1977, has made it into interstellar space, is the farthest manmade object in space and carries an invitation to any aliens who might find it!

✦ **Our galaxy spins at 140mph and travels through space at 190mph. This means we're all travelling at 330mph – so in one minute you are about 12,000 miles away from where you were!**

✦ **A teaspoon of neutron star material weighs about 110 million tons!**

✦ Every year the moon moves about 3.8cm further away from the Earth, so we're slowing by 0.002s per day.

The density of Saturn is so low that if you could put it in a giant glass of water, it would float

Ready Made Family!

An abandoned baby brings new life and meaning into the broken lives of Doreen and her friend, Jim

By Roberta Grieve

Doreen glanced out of the window, smiling as Jim the postman leaned his bicycle against the fence and opened her front gate. She had started looking forward to the post these days. She opened the front door just as Jim was about to knock.

"London postmark I see," he said, handing her the flimsy envelope.

"It's from Freddie." Doreen tore it open. "And there's a note from his mother still apologising for taking the children away."

"Can't blame her really. After all, there's been no bombs so far," Jim said, shouldering his bag. "Best be off – I'll see you on duty tonight."

Doreen went indoors to read the letters properly, picturing the children – Freddie, with his badly cut hair sticking up everywhere, and Lily, his shy little sister.

Doreen's fiancé had been killed in the Great War, and she had resigned herself to life without love – romantic love at least. Caring for her father until his death last year had been a labour of love of course, but she had to admit it hadn't been the sort of life she'd have chosen. Then the children had arrived, bringing unexpected sunshine into her life. They kept her so busy she no longer dreaded getting up in the morning, wondering how to fill the long empty hours ahead.

Mrs Hanson, the billeting officer, had voiced her doubts about Doreen's ability to cope with one child, let alone two. "You've no experience of young children, Miss Williams," she said.

Yet the tear-stained brother and sister in their shabby clothes, gas masks over their shoulders, labels attached to their coats as if they were parcels, were the only ones left in the village hall. The billeting officer had shrugged, "There's no-one else, so you'll have to take them."

Despite her misgivings, Doreen had gritted her teeth and resolved to do her best. "I'll manage," she said.

She took their hands and, murmuring encouragingly, had led them down the lane to her cottage. To her surprise, the children settled in quite quickly and she found herself enjoying the experience of looking after them. Once their initial shyness had worn off, they had chattered on about their life in London. Even Lily, who still sometimes cried for her mother at night, had begun to open up.

Continued overleaf

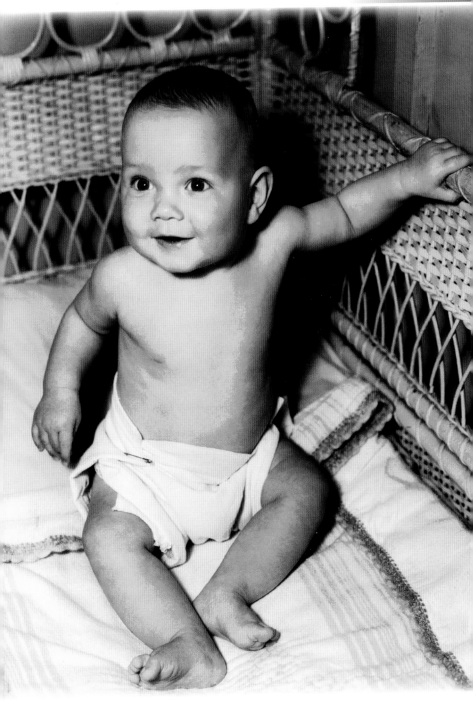

Continued from previous page

It was the baby chicks that did it. One day, Doreen had gone to fetch the eggs and found Lily sitting in the henhouse holding one of the fluffy little chicks in her palm and chatting away to it.

From then on, Lily seemed to take to country life. Freddie, her older brother, made friends with one of the farm lads and was always off roaming the woods and playing down by the stream.

It was a severe blow when one day the children's mother appeared on the doorstep demanding that they return to London with her. "It was all a false alarm," she said.

that when the war was over she'd invite them all for a holiday.

It was small comfort as she gloomily contemplated the empty day ahead. She decided to make a cake. Despite rationing, she still had plenty of ingredients in the larder and had hardly touched her sugar ration. It would kill time until she went on duty that evening.

She tried to suppress the thought that she wasn't baking the cake for herself, but Jim had no-one to cook for him now and she was sure he would enjoy a slice of her fruit cake.

She felt guilty for looking forward to the coming night's fire-watching at the top of the

Doreen's cheeks grew warm as she realised she had been thinking about Jim again

"There's been no air raids and things are back to normal. I miss my kids and their place is at home with me."

Doreen couldn't argue with that and she went upstairs to pack their few things, but she couldn't believe the pain she'd felt when they said goodbye.

Needing to fill the lonely hours after their departure she volunteered for fire watching duty. The village wasn't that far from Bristol and, despite what some were now calling the " phony war", the powers that be were still worried about possible bombing raids. That was how she'd got to know Jim – they shared the evening shift on top of the church tower three nights a week. But she still missed the children.

Now, re-reading Freddie's letter, she comforted herself that they must miss her too, or they wouldn't still write. Freddie's notes were misspelt with many crossings out and his mother's weren't much better, but it was nice they kept in touch. Doreen resolved

church tower. She wasn't supposed to enjoy it, she told herself, but she couldn't deny that life had improved since she'd got to know Jim.

Through the long dark nights, leaning on the parapet of the church tower, sharing a flask of tea, Jim had opened up, speaking affectionately of Rose, his late wife. "I miss her. We were together a long time," he said. "Rose and me had our ups and downs, but it was a good marriage. The pity was we never had kiddies."

Doreen's chance of marriage and family had been swept away in the chaos of the Somme, but she had buried her pain and got on with things. Now, for the first time, she talked about Henry, and the bitterness began to melt away. Jim's friendship and their shared affection for those two little evacuees had helped.

Doreen's cheeks grew warm as she realised she was thinking about Jim again. How foolish! Rose had only been gone a couple of years and he was still grieving. She gave herself a mental shake and filled the flask with tea, sweetened as Jim liked it. She didn't take sugar and there was plenty left after her baking session. She packed sandwiches and two slices of the fruit cake into her basket, adding gloves and a scarf in case it turned cold.

Inside the church was the familiar smell of old hymn books and lavender polish. A noise startled her. She swung her torch, its beam settling on a cardboard box from which came a feeble cry.

Doreen put down her basket and lifted the bundle out of the box, turning round as Jim's voice came out of the darkness.

"What've you got there, Doreen?"

"A baby. Poor little mite." Doreen rubbed the baby's back.

"We ought to report it – what about Mrs Hanson, the billeting officer?"

"We can't disturb her at this time of night." Doreen thought for a moment, then put a hand on Jim's arm. "You carry on without me. I'll take the baby home. Maybe you could call in at Mrs Hanson's in the morning – she'll know what to do."

"Sure you can cope?"

"Quite sure. I managed two children until recently, remember." She adopted a brisk, no-nonsense tone. "I'll be fine, Jim. Now get up in that tower and do your duty." She picked up the basket she'd prepared earlier. "Take this," she said.

Wondering what she'd let herself in for, she hurried away, the precious bundle carefully cradled in her arms.

When Jim called early next morning, she was coaxing the baby to suck from a piece of muslin stuffed in the neck of a milk bottle. She'd been a nervous giving him ordinary milk but he seemed to like it.

"What did Mrs Hanson say?" Doreen asked, as Jim gazed at the baby, a foolish grin on his face.

"She'll call in later this morning."

Mrs Hanson was closely followed by the Vicar and Constable Johnson, the village policeman. There hadn't been so many people in Doreen's parlour since her father had died. After so long keeping herself to herself, it was all rather overwhelming, but as she bustled around making tea she realised she was enjoying it. The baby slept on, unaware his future was being discussed.

"I think he should go to the orphanage in town," bossy Mrs Hanson said.

"Suppose his mother comes back? She won't know where he is," Doreen protested.

"She should've thought of that before leaving him." Mrs Hanson screwed her mouth up as if she were sucking a lemon.

The Vicar was more compassionate. "I'll leave a note on the church door saying he's being looked after and to contact me for any further information."

Constable Johnson coughed. "That's all very well, your reverence," he said. "But abandoning a baby is a crime."

"I appreciate that, but I think we should let Miss Williams look after him for the time being," said the Vicar. "Naturally, if I find out

Continued overleaf

Continued from previous page

anything, I'll let you know."

To Doreen's relief, the Vicar won the argument and it was decided the baby could stay with her while inquiries were made, although she could tell that Mrs Hanson wasn't happy at being over-ruled.

"If you're sure you don't mind, Miss Williams," said the constable.

"I'm only doing my duty," Doreen said.

They left, still debating hotly. Jim finished his tea and declared that he must go too. "Better get on with my post round."

As Doreen washed up the cups and tidied the kitchen, Henry – as she'd decided to name him – began to stir. She'd have to feed him soon. She'd also have to get a proper bottle, napkins, talcum powder – the list was endless. How would she get to the shops?

News had spread round the village, however, and for the rest of the morning Doreen was inundated, each visitor bringing "something for the baby" and wanting a peek at him.

Someone offered a pram, and there were outgrown baby clothes, tins of milk powder, bottles and teats – not to mention lots of useful advice.

"It's so kind, but I won't need all this," Doreen protested. She'd only have Henry for a few days… but the days turned to weeks, then months.

Inquiries by the village constable and appeals in the local paper brought no news of the baby's mother.

Doreen was so busy she didn't have time to miss Lily and Freddie, although she still looked forward to their letters and answered them straight away. Lily sent her a drawing of a baby in a cardboard box and Freddie was pleased it was a boy as "girls are boring".

When the first bombs fell on London a few weeks later, the children's mother wanted Doreen to have them again, but Mrs Hanson declared that it was impossible now she had the baby to care for. Doreen, however, surprised herself by standing up to the bossy older woman.

"You were glad enough to foist them on me when no-one else would take them," she said. "Besides, I know their little ways and their mother is happy for me to have them."

As she said later to Jim, who'd come round for Sunday tea, "We'll be like a proper family, won't we?"

"A proper family, eh?" Jim mused, chucking Henry under the chin. "I like the sound of that." Henry, who'd just begun to sit up, gurgled and chuckled. Jim turned to Doreen with a smile. "Seems he likes the sound of it, too," he said, putting his arms around her. "What about it, love? A proper family needs a father…"

"I think I like the sound of that too," said Doreen, raising her face for a kiss.

THE AUTHOR SAYS…

"When researching my novels I often come across stories which do not fit into the current novel. A newspaper snippet about an abandoned baby gave me the idea for Doreen and Jim's story."

Brain BOOSTERS

Kriss Kross

Try to fit all the listed words back into the grid.

4 letters	Inapt	7 letters	8 letters	9 letters
Lane Soda	Thumb	Liturgy	Literate	Brigadier
Ludo	**6 letters**	Lobelia	Lollipop	Light year
5 letters	Artist	Piebald	Nearside	Variation
Balti	Outing	Slavery		
Human	Retire			

For Better, For. . .

What was this peculiar attraction about the state of matrimony anyway? Maggie couldn't understand it

By Helen M Walters

I held the piece of paper in my hand for a long moment. It looked so formal. So legal, and final, and… well, absolute.

They say marriage is just a piece of paper, and now it turns out that divorce is as well. It's just a different sort of piece of paper. And it doesn't have all the other shenanigans attached to it. No cake, no confetti, no bridesmaids: just a piece of paper in an envelope on the doormat.

To say that my feelings were mixed as I looked at it would be an understatement. But then, my feelings on marriage have always been a bit all over the place.

"No daughter of mine is going to live in sin," my dad had said the first time Dean and I mentioned moving in together.

I was surprised he didn't say "over the brush". That's how old-fashioned he was. I stifled a giggle at the thought and his face registered an even higher degree of crossness under his eyebrows.

Mum talked him round in the end. "Och, all the youngsters do it nowadays," she said. "Maggie knows what she's doing. And isn't Dean a fine young man?"

There was no arguing with that, even for my dad, and he eventually accepted the situation.

It wasn't until I was pregnant with Bethan that it all started up again. And this time Mum joined in.

"Surely you're not going to have a child out of wedlock?" she said.

"Oh, Mum! It's not the 1950s," I responded. "No one cares about that now."

Mum just sniffed. A bigger sniff with each child that came along until we had three: Bethan, Will and then little Jack.

But Dean and I were happy as we were and at no point did the children ever experience anything other than a stable, loving family unit. That was all that mattered to me.

I still don't know what changed. It wasn't seeing my friends get married at increasingly glamorous and over-the-top venues. I'm not that shallow. And as my confirmed singleton mate, Susie, always said, you don't need to get married to throw an ace party.

It wasn't the frustration of explaining for the hundredth time that I was a Casey, and Dean and the children were Blythes.

Continued overleaf

Continued from previous page

I'd got that off pat a long time ago. It was just a nameless feeling, which I probably should have kept quiet about. But I didn't.

"Dean," I said one day, "I was wondering if we should get married after all."

"What's your dad said now?" Dean asked as he ironed the children's clothes for the next morning. He always was better at that kind of thing than me.

"Nothing," I said. And it *was* nothing. At least, nothing I could put my finger on.

and round on her finger. There was something about the way she clung to that ring in her grief that made me think my parents had experienced something deeper than I could begin to understand.

"I don't know what I'm going to do without the old grouch," she said.

Dad wasn't always the easiest person in the world to get on with, but I knew I'd never have another. And as for Mum, she looked like someone had turned the lights off in her eyes.

"I couldn't ask you, could I?" countered Susie. "What would Dean think?"

I tried to put it into words.

"We're settled, aren't we? We have three kids and we've decided we don't want any more. So what's next? I look into the future and I don't know what I see any more."

"That doesn't make any sense," Dean said, squirting steam at the collar of Bethan's school blouse. "You said it yourself. We're happy as we are. Why would we want to change? If it ain't broke, don't fix it."

And, of course, he was right. We couldn't just get married on the strength of an odd feeling I had.

Then my dad died and everything changed. My mum's world came crashing down around her, and mine shifted on its axis in sympathy, somehow making me feel rootless.

It was the effect on my mum that really made me think, though. As I poured her yet another cup of tea on the day after the funeral, she sat opposite me at the kitchen table and twisted her wedding ring round

"You've still got us, Mum," I soothed as I drank my tea and tried to hold back my own tears.

"I know, love. And I'm really grateful to you and Dean for everything you've done. But your dad was my life. He was…" She stopped and searched for the right word. "He was my *husband*."

After that, I did have words to express what I meant.

In the end, Dean proposed. Even though I knew he was only doing it to please me, the experience was still intoxicating. He went down on one knee, no less, and held out a solitaire engagement ring. I thought about that wedding ring, still firmly on Mum's finger even though Dad was gone. And I said yes.

Bethan was thrilled to be a bridesmaid.

"I look like a princess, don't I?" she said over and over again as she twirled around the hotel foyer before the service.

The boys were a bit too young to really enter into the spirit of it, but they seemed happy enough and in the photos, we're all smiling and looking forward to the future.

Mum had tears in her eyes when she kissed me and wished me luck.

"You've done the right thing," she said. "I hope you'll be every bit as happy as I was with your father."

There was no reason why we shouldn't have been happy. We already had the lovely home that so many couples have to fight for. We had three gorgeous, healthy children, and I knew how blessed that made us. And now we were married.

At first I enjoyed the novelty of being called Mrs Blythe. It really did make life easier to have the same name as the children. But after a few months the novelty of that wore off.

Then I noticed a subtle change in people's attitudes to me. People knew I was proud of my independence, but suddenly they started asking if Dean minded me doing things, as if they felt I now needed his permission.

It all came to a head when my best friend Susie wanted someone to go away for a weekend with her at short notice because she'd been let down by a not-very-reliable boyfriend yet again.

"I can't believe you didn't ask me," I said as we chatted in my kitchen.

"Well, I couldn't ask you, could I?" she countered. "What would Dean think?"

"The same as he thought the last time you asked me to go for a girly weekend away," I said with a shrug.

"But it's different now," Susie said, twisting her wine glass in her hands.

"Why's it different?" I asked, confused.

"Because you're married," she said.

I couldn't believe that even Susie thought such a thing, and it brought everything home to me. Despite what I'd thought about the supposed advantages of marriage, finally having the label of "wife" had made me feel trapped.

That wasn't the worst thing, though. That was the change in my relationship with Dean. I don't think it was his fault, and I don't think it was totally my fault either, but somehow we did start to take each other for granted. It started with an argument about the ironing.

"But you've always been better at it than me," I said, as he moaned about the huge pile that had built up.

"That doesn't mean I want to do all of it while you sit with your feet up watching television," he said with a huge sigh as he got the iron out.

We'd never argued about silly things like that before, but it felt as if that first niggle opened the floodgates and we couldn't stop having a go at each other about things we'd been happy to just get on with in the past. Eventually I started to get really worried about the children. It wasn't good for them to hear us bickering and having a go at each other all the time. The atmosphere in the house had gone from harmonious and relaxed to argumentative and stressful and I didn't know how to reverse it.

Underlying that, I still had the feeling of being trapped. My friends weren't asking me out as much – I wasn't sure whether that was because I was married, or because I'd turned into as big a grouch as my dad had been.

Continued overleaf

Continued from previous page

Finally, I had to accept it wasn't working. Just because marriage had been the right thing for my parents, that didn't mean it was the right thing for me.

By then we both realised we had to do something for the sake of our sanity and the children's happiness, so when Dean offered to go back to his parents' to give me some space, I agreed. I still loved him, but I couldn't live like that any more.

So, as I stood with the decree absolute in my hand that morning, I couldn't help wondering what it had all been about. We'd spent so long happily unmarried, then as soon as we became husband and

"No, but I still love you and we obviously can't stay away from each other."

"No." He gave me a lecherous grin as he stroked my bare leg.

"So what are we going to do?" I asked.

"Hmmm. Well, since you ask…" He fondled my knee.

"I'm being serious," I protested.

"So am I," he said, swapping his lecherous face for an earnest one. "The thing is, we're rubbish at marriage, but we love each other. So let's stay divorced, but stay together."

As I thought about it, I realised he was right. We'd never needed to be married. We weren't my parents; we were us.

"So, let me get this clear – you're

"The thing is, we're rubbish at marriage but we love each other. So…"

wife it had all seemed to fall apart.

I put the letter in my dressing gown pocket and headed upstairs. I didn't know what to do or what to feel about the letter, but I did know I wanted to go back to bed.

The children were all still asleep, so I crept into my room. It was only as I got into bed that the sleeping form under the duvet on the other side stirred a little.

No words greeted me, just a grunt, so I took the letter out and threw it at him.

"Look what was in the post," I said, wanting to know what he thought about it.

He rubbed sleepy eyes, smoothed out the letter and read it.

"So we're divorced, then?"

"Yes, Dean," I said, just as he began to shake with laughter.

"Well, we never were much good at being married, were we?" he said.

asking me to be your ex-wife?" I asked.

"Yes, I'm asking you to be happily divorced from me for the rest of our lives. Will you?" he asked, slipping out of the bed and getting down on his knees on the rug with a silly grin on his face.

I hesitated. I'd got this wrong before, horribly wrong, but the one thing I was certain of now was that I needed Dean to stay in my life for ever.

"Absolutely," I said.

● ●

THE AUTHOR SAYS…

"This story was inspired by thinking about relationships, and about how what works for some people doesn't work for everyone. Maggie has some difficult decisions to make before she finds what she needs."

The Long Walk

What happens when a father is determined his boy will *not* follow in his own impulsive footsteps?

By Beth Felix

Lyn wasn't sure who looked more excited – little Danny or Jack –when Jack hefted the five-gallon pan to the kitchen and set it on the stove.

Just days before, Jack had networked his way through his friends to land a new job at a local car factory. Lyn decided he deserved a little reward for that, so she'd given him a slap-up meal at the café where she worked – and now this.

"Right," Jack said to his little boy. "Danny, we're going to make some wort."

Danny bugged out his eyes and asked, "Is that French?"

Jack laughed.

"You might have to wait a few years to try what wort turns into, Danny. It's beer. I bet by the time you're old enough to drink it, I'll be a connoisseur. Now that's French."

Danny settled on a seat at the kitchen table to watch as Jack filled the huge pan full of water and let it heat. At just the right temperature, he added a muslin bag full of grains from the kit they'd bought.

"Now we have to wait," he said. "Thirty minutes for it to steep."

When its time was up, he pulled out the bag. Next he added thick malt extract from a plastic jar and stirred it in. Then he brought it all up to a rolling boil. A malty, sweet scent filled the house.

That's how Lyn remembered the early years of Jack's new hobby when Danny was just a little boy. In those days, he'd climb Jack's skinny ribs like a ladder, kiss his stubble-darkened cheeks and lace his fingers into his dark hair. Then he'd settle on Jack's lap to listen to another of his dad's tall tales.

"Be the best you can ever be. Then you won't need home-made beer," Jack told him by the stove. "You'll have champagne and a yacht and a huge big house somewhere **Continued overleaf**

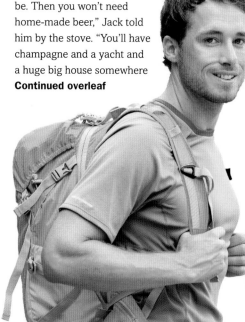

Continued from page 69

posh." That sweet rolling boil of their lives had lasted for years.

Jack could make beer blindfolded by the time fourteen-year-old Dan (no longer Danny) led a dark-skinned girl holding an armful of books into the kitchen.

After the stage of the sweet, rolling boil, there comes a time in beer-making when hops are added for flavour.

That was what Jack was doing the day Dan added a tiny bit more flavour to his young life.

The girl smiled at Jack and said, "My dad is a real-ale fan. He drinks Old Abbey Ale from a local brewery."

life. Then there were his male friends – noisy Tom, serious Gunther, shy Amare.

"I don't remember having so many friends when I was his age," Jack said to Lyn when Dan finally ushered the girl up to his room so they could study.

"He's becoming more sociable, Jack."

"Well, so long as they're helping with his work," he'd replied. "I don't want him to waste his life."

Perhaps Dan's future wouldn't have felt so important to him if they'd had another child, but that wasn't meant to be.

Beer must cool before you move it to its fermentation vat. If it's too hot, you kill the yeast. Sometimes icy blasts

"Bangkok to Singapore, San Francisco to New York. Fliss is planning it all..."

Jack, thicker-set these days, beamed at that. He pointed to the books she held.

"So you're studying physics, are you, and chemistry?"

He hid his calloused hands away. When the car factory had laid him off he'd found work with a road crew. He poured bitumen into potholes and resurfaced roads, sometimes overnight.

"Have you come to do some studying?" he asked the girl.

"I'd like to watch, if that's alright," she said, adding brightly, "What's next?"

"You put in a muslin bag full of hops and boil them for an hour. You can add more types, for added flavour, if you like, in the last fifteen minutes."

Like Sunila, red-haired Tracy, or delicate Ling before her, this new girl would definitely add more flavour to Dan's

from Siberia help the process.

"What, you're not going to university?"

There was something of a chilly, ill wind blowing on the day Jack stood all set to add a packet of yeast to the container that stood in the hall cupboard. He was barely concentrating on his batch of beer this time as Dan, now eighteen, paced back and forth.

"I'm planning to take a gap year, Dad. To travel – Bangkok to Singapore, Sydney to Auckland, San Francisco to New York. Fliss is planning it all."

"Fliss? Who's Fliss?"

"A girl I met last month when I was in the café with Mum. Fliss travels a lot. She's thinking of –"

"No!" Jack snapped, glaring at his son. "You already have a place at university.

Continued overleaf

It's all set. You don't want to end up like me, do you?" He worked in a warehouse now, driving a forklift truck. "Well, do you? Always cutting corners, always taking the cheapest option? You don't want a life like that."

Dan frowned, then turned for the door.

"Where are you going?" Jack demanded. "We need to talk."

The house felt as cold as ice that day as Lyn stared at the stubborn jut of her husband's jaw. "It's only for a year, Jack."

"No, it'll start with a year but it won't end at that. This is when he'll begin to think he can do whatever he likes and still get everything he wants."

Jack finally dumped the yeast into the jar and watched it sink down and down to the bottom of the murky liquid.

For two weeks the beer would be fermenting. She'd suspected Jack would be fermenting for far longer than that.

H e's taken a detour to Düsseldorf," she said when another postcard arrived. After a year and a half, the shoebox she kept under her bed upstairs overflowed with letters and cards.

Jack sat at the kitchen table trying to outstare his morning toast.

"He says he's moving on to France for the grape-picking season. You did that didn't you, when you travelled over there when you were young?"

Jack's chair scraped as he stood up.

"I should never have told him all those stupid stories about how I used to travel."

"But you had fun, didn't you? Working your way round the world."

"I filled his head full of rubbish," Jack snapped. "And I wasn't clever, the way he is. I had nothing to throw away. I knew if

he started travelling he'd never stop."

The back door slammed at Jack's back. He'd go into his shed and bottle up his latest batch of beer.

When Dan left, he'd thrown himself into his hobby. He might as well call himself a brewery now. His shed heaved with grains and special hops, dispatched in vacuum-sealed packets. He made beer now to his own recipes from scratch.

Every summer he'd invite half the street round to try it, while burgers sizzled on the brick barbecue he'd built.

This year, he'd talked about his latest job at the local college as a caretaker. He remained silent on his youthful adventures. Some of the teenagers present with their parents might hear him, after all, and he'd worry that wanderlust would ferment in their minds.

Now, in the kitchen, Lyn stared down at the postcard she held. It would have been nice if Jack would read just one, or answered Dan's calls, but Jack had his own special recipe for disapproval, too.

Winter arrived. You could bottle it in snow-globes, like the one Dan had sent from Switzerland where he'd been working as a waiter in a ski resort.

In Lyn's street, everything stood white and gleaming. Jack was in his shed, printing his own labels. Robin Red Breast's Tipple, The Snowman's Ale, and Jingle All the Way Home would be given away at Christmas time.

Dan's letter trembled in Lyn's hands.

Hi Mum, I'm guessing Dad isn't reading anything I write. I expect he thinks Fliss is pregnant by now and I'll come home looking for a job to support us. That's how it happened for you two,

a café I meet a pregnant girl some rat has abandoned?"

"Just tell him," Lyn insisted. "Tell him."

She pushed him inside the shed. She almost felt she should hold the door shut in case this boiling brew bubbled over.

The air stilled. She listened hard until she heard the words Dan had also written in his letter.

"I'm off to university next year."

He looked just like his dad in those sweet, malty years. He laughed as he held her

isn't it, when you met at the café?

The way he goes on you'd think he'd made an awful mess of his life. I hear him when I'm talking to you on the phone, you know. I hear him grumbling about everything I'm throwing away. You believe in me still, don't you, Mum?

Oh yes, Lyn thought, *but I've had a lot of practice.*

Mum, he'd added. *I'm coming home.*

There wasn't any fanfare to announce his homecoming that day. Not even a chime of the front doorbell. She saw instead his shadow pass the kitchen window and she raced to the back door.

It took her a second to take him in. The shadow of a beard, the floppy hair: he looked just like his dad in those sweet, malty years. She flung her arms about him. He laughed as he held her.

"I love you, Mum," he said.

Without a word, she turned him about and pushed him towards the shed.

"Let your dad get a look at you… then tell him what you've got planned."

"You mean travelling on a shoestring for the rest of my life? At least until in

All the beer you've made, Jack, she thought. *Yet you never seemed to realise some things need more time to mature. Dan's like you. He won't wander off again now his mind's made up. You could have left us a hundred times, but you never did.*

She heard the clank of two bottles meeting in a toast and heard Jack laugh.

She remembered him the very first day they'd met, in the café where she still worked. It stood two streets from the docks. He'd carried in a holdall that day and smiled at her. Noticed her bulging stomach and frowned.

At the counter, he'd made small talk. He was twenty-eight and working his way round the world. "I love travelling," he'd said. "Nothing's going to stop me."

"Oh, you never know," she'd replied, smiling into his twinkling blue eyes. "One day, you might find something – or someone – you love even more."

THE AUTHOR SAYS…

"Inspired by my late mother's love of making not beer but wine. She became quite an expert over the years."

Bye Bye Barbie

My ruthless grown-up daughter was all too ready to throw out her childhood dolls. Only I wasn't!

By Angela Pickering

My daughter was having a clear-out that day. She was better at it than I; more ruthless. She waved a Barbie doll at me by its legs and grinned.

"This one can go as well," she announced cheerfully.

I sighed. There was a pile of shapely figures already on the carpet by my feet. Then there was the toy wardrobe with its delicate drawer full of dolls' underwear

I picked up one blonde figure and fiddled with her shoes. One was falling off and I couldn't take her to the charity shop improperly dressed.

"Oh, Mother," Alice said. "Stop playing with the dolls and help me."

I packed the dolls, books and other knick-knacks Alice handed to me into black bin liners. I put the bags in the hall ready to go next time I went into the village.

"Now, don't you forget, Mum." Alice

"Oh, Mother," Alice said. "Stop playing with the dolls and help me out with this"

and shoes. *How could Alice possibly part with them?* I wondered.

I shouldn't have been surprised really; she'd never been keen on dolls. She was more into her teddy bears, fluffy bunnies and toy cats than dressing up dolls.

Maybe I'd been wrong to assume that my daughter would like the things I liked. But surely, you'd think that every little girl would like dolls.

said, "I don't expect to see them still here next time I come round." She shook a finger under my nose. "I know you too well."

"That's all very well," I replied, "but all of these things are part of my life too, you know – not just yours."

I don't think she understood how many memories the toys conjured up for me.
Continued overleaf

When she'd gone back to her new flat, I sat in her old room and reminisced. She'd been such a sweet child, despite not loving the dolls as much as I did.

I suppose I almost bought them for myself. I was too old by the time Barbie was invented to have one, so I made the most of Alice's. I'd only had one doll as a child. I named her Mollie after my sister and she named hers after me.

My doll was still in the loft, together with the little outfits I'd made her once I'd learnt how to sew.

Different things gave us pleasure when I was a girl. Mollie and I had loved to sew – we made clothes for ourselves as well as for our dolls. Sometimes all four of us wore matching outfits.

"Hey, Sue, what're you doing up there?"

Trevor, my husband, had arrived home from work while I'd been lost in the past.

"I could have a study in here, you know."

"I was thinking of a sewing room."

"You don't sew."

"I might if I had a sewing room."

I could always make him laugh.

He knew I'd been a bit of a seamstress in my youth, but life with two children had filled my world with other things.

"We should do something with the room, though," he continued. "It's too nice to leave empty."

He was right. It was a lovely room, overlooking the garden and catching all the early-morning sun. Even during the evenings there was a comfortable feeling in the room, as if serenity had been built into the walls along with the plaster.

"Let's get a takeaway," I suggested, at last, in case he'd noticed that I'd been too busy day-dreaming to organise any dinner.

"Been too busy with this lot to cook, have you?" he said, grinning.

My sister was right, I was a hoarder – but I knew she had a doll called Susan in her loft

He clomped up the stairs as if carrying a heavy weight.

"I found these in the hall," he said, dumping two black bin bags on the bed.

I couldn't help laughing.

"They're for the charity shop," I said. "Alice has had a clearout."

"Has she been round, then?" His face dropped.

"Don't worry; she's coming back in a day or two." I looked at the bags. "I'd better take these into the village quick smart, or I'll be in trouble."

He gazed around the empty room.

"Looking on the bright side," he mused,

That night I couldn't sleep. My head was filled with memories and my feet were restless, as if I were working on Mum's ancient treadle sewing machine.

I slipped out of bed so as not to disturb Trevor and wandered into Alice's room. I had offered to let her take the bed, but she'd said she wanted a new one.

"We should get rid of this," said Trevor, wandering in behind me and flopping down on the bed next to me. "It's just taking up room."

"Can't you sleep either?" I said.

"I ate too much," he said ruefully, rubbing his stomach.

"Now there are only the two of us, we should take up some new hobbies," I suggested, trying to take his mind off the discomfort. "Healthy ones – like jogging or weight training."

"I was thinking more of stamp collecting," he said, "now that I'm to have a study."

"You don't collect stamps," I felt obliged to mention.

"But I might if I had a study."

The next day I met up with Mollie, in the local charity shop. She'd been running the place for several years. She took my bag of bits from me with a knowing smile.

"Having a clearout, now they've all gone?" she enquired.

"Not my choice," I replied. "Alice thought she was helping."

Mollie chuckled. "You've always been a bit of a hoarder," she said.

I knew she was right, but as I looked around the shop, I still saw quite a few bits and pieces I wanted to buy to fill up the empty spaces at home. I also knew that

she had a doll called Susan in her loft, so I wasn't the only hoarder in the family.

"Now you haven't got so much on," Mollie continued, as if she were psychic, "you're going to need a new hobby."

"I'll give it some thought," I said.

A lice was full of suggestions next time she called.

"Dad will be retiring next year. He'll need a new hobby too," she said.

"He's thinking of philately," I said, just to watch her eyebrows shoot up. They did.

She patted the bed. "If it's all right, I might just take this after all," she said. "For my spare room."

"Of course," I said. "I've got some ideas for the room anyway."

Three weeks later the room had been transformed. We'd painted it in neutral colours and I was waiting for the desk I'd ordered as a surprise for Trevor to be delivered. I wasn't sure if he'd been serious about the stamp collecting, but the

Continued overleaf

album hadn't cost much and a couple packets of foreign stamps from Amazon hadn't broken the bank either.

At last a huge delivery van pulled up outside. Trevor had the day off, so it was surprise time. His mouth dropped open as his new desk and chair were man-handled up the stairs.

Then mine dropped open as my new sewing table and machine went up after it.

"And I bought you these," I managed to say and I handed him the stamp album and stamps.

A lice was delighted with what we'd done with her room.

"So what are you going to make, Mum?" she said, after having a go on my lovely new sewing machine.

She'd spotted the bin bag, where ten young ladies waited for their new dresses

"Dolls' clothes," I said, "for the charity shop. It's your Auntie Mollie's idea; she's giving me the material cut from donated clothes that won't sell."

"What a brilliant idea. What a shame we got rid of all those Barbies."

"Well, actually," I began and then saw the twinkle in her eye.

Of course she'd spotted the bin bag in the corner, where ten young ladies waited for their new dresses.

"So you get to play with dolls again," she said after we'd giggled for a while.

"And *then*, once each one has a whole new wardrobe, they're going to the charity shop."

"And how's Dad getting on with the stamp collecting?"

"Oh, he's given that up," I replied. "He's having a go at writing a novel instead. He said now that he's got a study he should make the most of it."

"So… what exactly have you donated to the charity shop instead of the dolls?" asked my persistent daughter.

"Mmm… nothing much so far," I admitted. "In fact, just a few stamps and a stamp album."

THE AUTHOR SAYS…

"I've always loved dolls. My daughter didn't. In the end I bought myself a Barbie or two – and why not? They're packed away in the loft now, the urge has been satisfied."

Strawberry Scones with Clotted Cream

Ingredients (Makes 12)

- ✦ **350g self-raising flour, plus extra for dusting**
- ✦ **¼tsp salt**
- ✦ **1tsp baking powder**
- ✦ **80g chilled butter, cut into pieces**
- ✦ **45g caster sugar**
- ✦ **175ml milk**
- ✦ **1tsp vanilla extract**
- ✦ **1tsp lemon juice**
- ✦ **1 small egg, beaten, to glaze**
- ✦ **Clotted cream and strawberry jam, to serve**

1 Preheat the oven to 220°C, Fan Oven 200°C, Gas Mark 7. Put a baking sheet on the middle shelf of the oven.

2 Sift the flour, salt and baking powder into a large bowl. Add the butter and rub it in with your fingertips until it looks like fine crumbs. Stir in the sugar.

3 Heat the milk until just lukewarm, then stir in the vanilla and lemon juice. Put to one side for a few moments. The mixture may curdle slightly.

4 Make a well in the flour mixture, add the milk and stir with a round-bladed knife (don't worry if it seems quite wet). Sprinkle a work surface with flour, and sprinkle a little over the dough and onto your hands. Knead the dough lightly and form into a circle, about 4cm thick.

5 Use a plain 5cm cutter to stamp out the scones, re-rolling the dough as necessary. Quickly arrange the scones on the hot baking sheet. Brush the tops with beaten egg, then bake for 10-12min until risen and golden. Serve warm, topped with clotted cream and strawberry jam.

Cook's tip: To give the scones a better rise, avoid twisting the cutter.

RECIPE AND FOOD STYLING: SUE ASHWORTH PHOTOGRAPHY: JONATHAN SHORT

First Love

Hairstyles change but emotional dilemmas span the generations, as Norman and young Jack discover

By Sarah Burbage

M orning, Mabel, love."
The first thing Norman did every morning was to say hello to his wife's photograph.

Mabel smiled out of an ornate frame on the bookcase.

"Do things that make you happy when I'm gone," she'd said to him the very last time he'd held her hand.

Norman hurried into the hall and picked up the post. He shuffled through the envelopes as he wandered back to the front window of his flat. Across the wide expanse of grass outside, an old ash tree stood bathed in sunlight. Norman smiled at it then let his mind wander back to a cold day a few months ago…

A boy sat under the ash with the hood of his sweatshirt pulled up to hide his face, his long fringe stuck out of it like stuffing exploding from a mattress.

Norman squinted. Was his hair purple? He huffed to himself. The youth of the day were such a strange bunch, all odd words and strange clothes.

One thing never changed, though. The boy scrambled to his feet as, down on the ribbon of pavement below, he spotted a girl – a girl who broke into a trot, then slowed herself right down, clearly worrying she might appear far too eager.

Norman stood smiling when she finally sauntered up to the boy. They didn't kiss or hold hands in greeting. No, this looked like a brand-new friendship. Like buds on an apple tree, it would take a lot more warmth before any blossom appeared.

The pair sat down and started to chat. They rocked back and forth as, in turns, they made each other laugh. They darted glances to each other's face when they thought the other wouldn't notice.

Norman watched it all with a smile. Then he told himself off for being such a nosy old fool. He went into his kitchen to make a sandwich for tea but couldn't resist peering through the blinds now and again to the ash tree and the young couple.

First love, he thought: it was so sweet and innocent, so hesitant and shy.

At dusk the couple parted. She went one way; he the other. They turned their heads now and again as they walked away, as if checking they weren't in the middle of a dream. Norman chuckled.

"They'll be back," he said, nodding the tree, sure that if the ash could, it would nod its leafy head right back. "Oh yes, they'll be back."

T hey were too – the very next evening and the one after that. Norman would catch little glimpses. The space between the girl and the boy narrowed. They

Continued overleaf

started to hold hands. He swore he saw their very first kiss.

He chuckled, his heart swelling, his eyes wandering to Mabel's picture.

"First love," he murmured pensively. "You never forget it."

The very next evening when Norman looked out at the tree, only the boy sat underneath it, the cool breeze rippling his white T-shirt. Norman glanced to his clock. The girl should be here by now.

Was it over so soon? He stared at the boy, taking in his sharp nose and blade-sharp cheekbones, wondering what girls saw in boys these days. Wasn't he handsome or clever enough?

He gave a dry swallow, seeing the boy on his phone. The boy's shoulders shook as he put it away and he swiped a wrist across his eyes.

Norman pushed his window open.

He'll tell you to mind your own business, you know.

"Why doesn't her dad like you, then?" Norman asked. The boy shrugged.

"I don't know. He just doesn't."

He knows alright, Norman thought, *but who would ever want to say out loud that somebody saw you as second-best?*

"Can't you go round and see her?" he asked encouragingly.

"No," the boy said and shook his head by way of emphasis. "I can't."

He daren't. He's too afraid.

"I understand. Been there myself. There's nothing worse than somebody looking at you as if you'd just crawled out from under a rock, now is there?" He gave a sympathetic smile. "But you can't just give up now, can you?"

The boy shrugged again, pushing back his fringe that stubbornly fell right into his eyes again. His hair likely didn't pass muster either with the girl's father.

"What happened to your…?" Norman waved at the boy's fringe.

"Oh, I like it purple."

"Her sister's keeping tabs on her. I don't want to get either of them into trouble"

"Is everything alright?" he asked as gently as he could. "Where's your friend today?"

He half-expected a rude rebuke. Instead, the boy gawped, shell-shocked either by his phone call or by Norman's sudden intrusion.

"Her… her dad won't let her see me anymore," he mumbled.

"Oh, I see." Norman hummed and glanced at Mabel's picture. "Well, that happens sometimes. It happened to me."

The boy stood up and edged closer.

I see. "Well, each to his own, that's what I say. Would you like a cup of tea?"

The boy thrust his hands in his pockets. He glanced about as if afraid he'd be caught talking to an old man through his window.

"How about a biscuit?"

The boy opened his mouth, then shrugged. One more glance to make sure they were alone and he nodded. "Thanks."

"What's your name?"

"Jack."

"I'm Norman." Norman offered his

hand. The boy peered suspiciously at him, then shook it. "Don't give up, Jack. Love takes courage."

Norman frowned, sure the boy's eyes had filled for a moment with some veiled emotion. It took the time for the kettle to boil for him to realise what it was. Relief.

Maybe no one else had ever told him not to give up. Maybe they'd simply pointed out that puppy love doesn't count for much.

Only, as Norman remembered it, love felt the same at any age.

The boy drank a cup of tea and ate three digestives. He leaned into the open window so Norman could sit down in his chair.

They talked about how Jack's friends were teasing him about his hair and how he thought he should dye it brown. How he lived with his mum and tried to help her out. How he'd started to meet Sara at lunchtimes at school too, before her dad had found out.

They talked about how Norman didn't get many visitors these days.

"You really need to go round, you know, and talk to Sara's father. Politely, of course," Norman told him as the wind stirred the leaves of the old ash.

Jack shook his head. No, he was too afraid of the man.

Norman watched him amble off home that day. Jack's shoulders nestled up about his ears, his face hidden away in his hood.

Norman imagined him growing up that way, shrunken and hidden, never straightening his back, sticking out his chest and feeling worthy of a little happiness.

The next day, Jack sat all alone under the ash tree once again.

He dialled his phone over and over, sitting there listening to it ring before turning it off. No answer. No reply.

Norman pushed his window open and set a tea cup on the sill with a plate of biscuits.

"No luck?" he asked when Jack hurried over. He shook his head. "Haven't you spoken to Sara at school at all?"

"Her sister's keeping tabs on her," Jack said, looking pale and shadow-eyed that day. "I don't want to get either of them into trouble."

"I see," Norman replied. "So, have you thought any more about going round to her house?"

With that, Jack wouldn't meet his gaze. He stared down at his grass-stained trainers instead.

The next evening was just the same. Jack was becoming an expert at waiting. He sat with his legs tucked against his ribs, his head down on his knees. At least until Norman opened his

Continued overleaf

window and waved him over.

"Do you really want to sit out there all evening, Jack, or do you want to come in?"

Jack's brow furrowed as if this tiny attempt at bravery might defeat him.

"I could come in, couldn't I?" he said as if persuading himself.

"Come on then. It looks like rain and there's no sense in you getting soaked."

"Do you think I'm being a coward?" Jack asked later, hunched over his mug in Norman's sitting room.

Norman glanced over to his precious picture of Mabel, then at the old fountain pen, the paper and envelopes he'd placed on the coffee table. *To gather dust*, he

to find the boy wide-eyed and panting.

"I did it! I did it! I went round to see Sara." His knees seemed to lock as he staggered inside.

"And?" Norman asked urgently.

"Her dad told me to go away. So I told him, politely just like you said, that I thought it'd be a good idea if he got to know me better. I told him how I help my mum and how one day I want to be a mechanic." Jack flopped into a chair, feeling at his chest as if his heart were about to fly right out of it. "Sara's mum was there. She told him he ought to show me the motorbike he was working on." Jack gave a crooked grin. "And then he did! We talked for ages after that."

His mobile rang. Nervous as a rabbit,

"Sara's mum told him he ought to show me the motorbike he's working on..."

thought wryly. He shook his head.

"I think you just need a bit of time to gather yourself. I believe in you, Jack."

Jack chewed his lip. "Really?"

Norman smiled. "I think you're a nice lad. Honest and decent. If I had a daughter, I'd have been happy to find you at my door."

Jack's cheeks flushed.

"Thanks," he said, before he smiled.

Now, weeks later, standing in his sunny hallway, Norman stared down at the envelopes in his hand.

He discarded three bills, then a glossy flyer. He came to a small white envelope and heaved in a slow breath.

He remembered the day Jack had pounded on his door. How he'd opened it

he answered it. His eyes widened.

"Sara? You can phone? Your dad says it's OK?" He twitched with excitement. "That's great. That's really great."

Norman had stood by, smiling. Now, alone, he turned the white envelope over.

He cleared his throat, puffed out his chest and set his shoulders straight. *You're worthy of a little happiness too, Norman.*

He pulled at the paper flap, shredding it in his haste into confetti. He opened up the letter inside and held his breath.

Dear Norman,

I was so surprised to hear from you after all these years. I think the post office redirected your letter three times before it finally found me.

Yes, I would like to see you. I'd love to remember the old days with you. I'm all

on my own now, too. I know you said you were nervous about writing but I'm so, so pleased you did.

Her name was Joyce. He'd kissed her under a different tree a very long time ago. Her dad had hated him, but he hadn't fought for her. He'd given up.

He'd heard later about her marriage and her children. Little snippets of her life had come and gone, meaning little then as a happily married man with a family of his own, but things were different now and first loves were never forgotten. They stayed in your heart forever.

He glanced across to Mabel's picture.

"Do things that make you happy when I'm gone," she'd said to him.

"I will, love," he said now as he held onto the letter. "I'll try."

He wandered over to the window and stared out at the old ash three. He smiled, knowing he would never have dared write to Joyce if he hadn't met young Jack. If he hadn't reminded them both of the simplest of truths: that love takes courage.

THE AUTHOR SAYS...

"Inspired by the scruffy young boy with green hair I saw meeting up with a very prim and polished young girl. It was definitely first love!"

Hands Off!

It was my first day in my new job, and the last thing I wanted to do was split up the workplace couple…

By Susan Wright

S o are you getting the hang of it all?" the landlord asked me just before the end of my shift.

"Yes – it's not as hard as I thought it would be," I replied. "I was terrified that people would ask for cocktails but nearly everybody's gone for beer."

Colin grinned. "Yes, well, most people aren't very adventurous, so getting the drinks isn't hard. Coping with some of the men can be a challenge, though."

"Mm, tell me about it," I replied, thinking that coping with Matt the barman had been even worse. "Some of them are a bit flirtatious."

"And others are very flirtatious," Colin said. "I heard a couple of things that were said and I thought you coped very well. It can be difficult. The girl you replaced left because she couldn't handle it."

"Oh, right," I said, raising my eyebrows. "Well, I can handle it."

"Yes, I'm sure you can," Colin said. "Anyway, just collect the empty glasses up and then you can go home, Bev."

"OK, thanks," I said, wondering if I'd be able to get to the end of my shift without Matt coming on to me again.

He'd been flirting with me ever since I'd turned up that evening. A couple of times he'd even touched me when he'd had to get past me behind the bar.

The feel of his hands on my hips had stirred up something inside me that had been lying dormant for years – but I hadn't responded because of something one of the barmaids had said when I'd first got the job.

"Just keep your hands off my Matt," she'd warned me after I'd come out of the room where I'd been interviewed.

"Oh right," I'd said. "Is he your husband, then?"

She'd shaken her head. "No, but hopefully he will be one of these days. I'm trying to pluck up the courage to propose, but I keep chickening out because some men have a problem with marriage, don't they?"

"Yes, they do," I'd agreed, remembering how my husband had had a massive problem with marriage and cheated on me more times than I cared to remember.

I'd thrown him out in the end, and I knew I'd done the right thing, but it had been difficult to cope financially so I'd applied for the job in the pub to get a bit more money.

My first evening had been easier than I'd expected – except for having to deal with Matt.

Continued overleaf

Continued from previous page

He'd made several complimentary comments about my appearance, and half way through the evening he'd even suggested we should go out sometime.

"No, I don't think so," I'd said.

He'd looked disappointed.

"Oh, have you got a partner, then?"

"No, but I'm off men," I'd replied.

"Oh, right," he'd said. "Still, you won't be off men forever, will you?"

"No, but it will be a while," I'd muttered, thinking how annoying it was that the first man I'd been drawn to for years was totally out of bounds.

He was really attractive, and as I collected the empty glasses up, I couldn't help thinking how excited I would be if he was available.

The first man I'd been drawn to in years – and he was totally out of bounds

"Right, I've finished," I announced to Colin once I'd put all the dirty glasses by the sink.

"OK, you can go, then," he replied. "It will be different bar staff tomorrow, so you'll have some new people to meet."

"OK," I said.

"Like Karen," he went on, his eyes twinkling. "And her boyfriend, Matt. You'd better keep your hands off him or she'll have your guts for garters!"

I frowned. "Matt?"

"Yes, the other Matt," Colin explained as the Matt I'd been working with walked up to us. "There are two Matts working here. It can get confusing, but you'll soon get used to it – and this Matt's single, aren't you, Matt?"

"Yes, but Bev's off men," Matt replied gloomily.

"But I won't be off them forever!" I blurted out before I could stop myself.

Matt's eyes lit up, then he gave a puzzled frown.

"But you said it would be a while."

"And it's been a while," I said, my heart doing a little dance as I grinned at him. "It's been a couple of hours at least!"

· ·

THE AUTHOR SAYS...

"I go to a pub quiz every Tuesday evening, and after chatting to a new barmaid one week, my mind started working overtime, and I came up with this story."

FANCY THAT!

Fascinating facts about **our seas**

A shrimp's heart is in its head

✦ Sea sponges have no head, mouth, eyes, feelers, bones, heart, lungs or brain – yet they ARE alive!

✦ Underwater hot springs that shoot water at an incredible temperature of 340°C – enough to melt lead – have a profusion of life around them.

✦ **14% of the world's protein consumption comes from fish.**

✦ Antarctica has as much ice as the Atlantic Ocean has water.

✦ **We have only explored 5% of the world's oceans and have better maps of Mars than of the ocean floors.**

✦ If you've ever swallowed a mouthful of seawater while swimming, you've also gulped around 1 million bacteria and hundreds of thousands of phytoplankton!

✦ **Sharks' skin feels like sandpaper because it is covered in "dermal denticles" which are really tiny teeth!**

✦ According to the World Register of Marine Species, as of Sept 2014, there are currently at least 226,408 named marine species.

✦ **Jellyfish have been around for more than 650 million years – they outdate both sharks and dinosaurs.**

In terms of legal jurisdiction, 50% of the United States lies under the ocean

✦ At 188 decibels, the song of the blue whale is the loudest sound made by any animal on the planet.

Oysters can change from one gender to the other – and back again – depending on which is best for mating

✦ **At depths where the pressure would be** enough to crush the Titanic like a drinks can, crabs, octopuses and tube worms calmly go about their daily lives.

✦ The largest mountain range in the world is underwater. The Mid-Oceanic Ridge runs for more than 35,000 miles, has peaks higher than the Alps, and comprises 23% of the Earth's surface.

The Way We Were

Now Dad was home, it seemed Mum had changed even more than he had…

By Alison Carter

"**A**udrey, will you get that?" Winny Bains called to her elder daughter. "My hands are all over suet!"

"Patty can go," Audrey called back.

"I asked you! For goodness' sake, Audrey, just open the door. Whoever it is will go away again."

Audrey scowled at her little sister, who was grinning stupidly. She put down her sketch book and stood up, her long, skinny legs unfolding like a pocket ruler, and shuffled into the hall.

She opened the front door. A dark-haired man in a loose-fitting suit stood there, holding a battered case. He looked vaguely familiar.

Continued overleaf

ILLUSTRATIONS: GETTY IMAGES, MANDY DIXON

"I'm sorry," the man said. He looked up and down the long street. His face showed puzzlement. "I think I've come to the wrong house."

Audrey was almost thrown aside by her mother rushing to the door.

"Charlie!"

The two grown-ups stood looking at each other for a second. The man dropped his case.

"Winny… love…"

She fell into his arms and he kissed her, holding her tightly, stroking her hair.

Seven-year-old Patricia ran towards the group along the narrow hallway. She stared at the embracing figures. Then the two sisters looked at one another. Patricia dashed back into the parlour and came back holding a small, framed photo.

"It's him," she whispered.

Two empty cups stood on the table.

"Girls! It's terrible in here." She looked suddenly harassed. "Today of all days! Clear it up, quickly!"

"Don't worry, love," he said, kissing her cheek. "Let my lovely girls draw. I always did. I'm going to put my kettle on in my kitchen and sit with my feet up on my table. It is the same table with the ring on it where you once put the pan down?"

She held up a scolding finger, smiling.

"You will certainly not put the kettle on. No work for you, Charlie Bains, just home from a war, for goodness' sake. I will make tea, and whatever to eat my husband's heart desires."

Most men had been home for leave at some time during that miserable conflict, but Audrey's father had not seen his family since 1939. Mother had talked

"Don't answer back. Your father's fought a war for you. He deserves the best"

The lovers drew apart and the man, who seemed to be their father, looked wonderingly at Audrey.

"It's you," he said, shaking his head. "I left a little girl of three and now look at her… and baby Patricia. My –"

"Patty," the little redhead said firmly.

"Patty, then. Whatever you like. Oh, it's good to be home. Here, don't I get a cuddle from my daughters?"

It was odd, being enfolded by the arms of this big, tall man. He smelled quite unlike her mother, and unlike home.

Then Mother took his hand and led him into the front room. The rug was awash with drawings and broken pencils.

and talked about his bravery, and here he was, their hero, in the flesh.

Mum laid the table in the front room. Audrey couldn't remember using that varnished table to eat at, not ever. It was for a "best" that never came. Apparently it had come today.

Mum was different somehow, too. She had done her hair, and she'd been beetling about like anything, chivvying Audrey and Patty to look nice, pull up their socks, get rid of the school books and the comics.

"Now, you can carve for us, love." Winny held out the knife as she approached from the sideboard, handle towards him. "The butcher did me a

favour when he heard. It's so good to have our man back to carve."

She smoothed her skirt and sat down.

"You look funny, Mum," Patty said.

"Whatever do you mean?" Mum said.

"Your back all stiff and straight. Like Miss Wenn at school."

"Don't be silly. It's a special occasion."

Father had bathed. He said it was his best bath ever, which made the girls laugh. Audrey liked him, and she began to gather together in her mind all the small flashes of memory she had of him. Hadn't he played with them in the back yard making mud pies? It seemed unlikely.

Now, he wore loose, comfortable-looking trousers and a sleeveless sweater over a shirt. The shirt sleeves were rolled up and she noticed a hole in one of them. He leaned back in his chair, sighing with what Audrey assumed was contentment. She couldn't really tell; she didn't know him.

"Are you alright wearing those old things, Charlie?" Mum asked awkwardly.

"I kept a nice blazer hanging in a laundry cover. You'd just bought it when you were called up. It's in the cupboard."

He rubbed the worn wool of the sweater, up and down on his broad chest. "I love this old thing," he said.

"Let's eat," Mum said.

"I'm starving," Patty said.

Mum frowned at her. "You know that Daddy's getting the lion's share of this, Patricia."

"I'm Patty."

"Don't answer back. Do you think your father's been living in luxury? He's fought a war for you. He deserves the best."

Father laughed.

"I can see you two need the nourishment," he said. "Growing girls."

Later, as they headed up the stairs to bed, Winny stopped her daughters for a moment. She stood below them, so her face was on a level with Audrey's.

"Try to behave well, girls," she said. "Your dad needs… he needs… easing in. We must keep the house nice, and show him how much better is it here than in a horrid war."

Audrey and Patty nodded, and turned to climb the stairs. Winny stayed at the bottom for a moment before going to join Charlie in the front room, tidying her hair with her hand.

Audrey had been to the pictures with her mother and sister, just before her father's return. There had seen a newsreel with a bit about the "homecoming serviceman". It showed the happiest of families – Dad in smart khaki, apple-cheeked mother in a flowery dress and high heels, matching boy and girl – all of them embracing together. The girl wore

Continued overleaf

an impossibly film-starrish dress, the pink skirt sticking out like a plate. There was a cottage with roses round the door and a white picket fence.

Mother had put an arm around her and Patty in the dark picture house, and whispered, "We'll make it just like this when Daddy gets back. We'll make it perfect."

Their house had no roses, Audrey thought, and the two children in the picture were perfect, rosy little things. Not like freckly Patricia, not like Audrey herself – thin, pale, gangly, nine years old.

Mother gave up her job at the War Bonds office soon after Father got back home.

"The work was a necessity," she said one morning, "while you were absent."

"You don't have to stop on my account," Father said, leaning across the small table and stroking her cheek. "Don't think everything has to alter." He chuckled. "Just act as though I'm not here."

Mother looked shocked.

"What a thing to say! You home at last, and all you can say is –"

"I didn't mean anything by it," he interrupted, calming her. "But I like slipping into your routine. You know, stand at ease, carry on."

Patty giggled.

"We want everything to be right for our returning hero," Mum said firmly, pouring him more tea. "Audrey, boil another kettle, will you? This pot is getting cold."

Audrey reflected that, before, they'd never minded warm tea.

Winny smiled at Father encouragingly. "Now you're working again, I can stay at home and make sure this place is just so."

"But you said you liked the War Bonds?" Father persisted.

"Well, I don't know about 'liked'. I think I've come to have an understanding of investments. I helped with poster campaigns, and ran local savings weeks in –"

"All over the county," Patty chipped in proudly. "What did the campaign say, Mum? 'Lend to Defend'."

Audrey nodded, chewing her bread.

"You said those slogans are branded on your forehead," she put in.

"Don't talk with your mouth full," Mum said. "I was… competent at the work."

"Well," Dad said, "you can keep on with it, if you like."

"I'll see," she said. "Now, girls, where are your satchels?"

Audrey and her sister were not exactly sure how to act around Father. He hurried in through the front door when he came back from work, eager to cuddle his children and ask about their day.

Mum would hurry too, taking his coat and settling him in a chair. She would have the girls bringing him a glass of beer, and then shoo them away to do homework or get ready for Brownies.

"It's very different, having a dad," Patty said one night as they lay in their beds.

"You've always had a father, stupid," Audrey said.

"I mean, having one in the house. Mum never used to worry about doing homework right now, and it's all so very tidy. I'm exhausted."

Audrey laughed. Her little sister could be very dramatic.

"I suppose things have to change," Audrey conceded.

"Does he want everything just so?" Patty asked, yawning, "Like Mum says."

"'Spose so. Now shut up and go to sleep, will you?"

The next day was Saturday, and warm. Patty wandered out into the back yard and found some bits of wood. Mother had been fretting about the mess, but hadn't had time to tidy. Audrey watched her sister making a den in a corner, against the fence. After half an hour she went out.

"You'll have to make it stronger than that," she said. "When you put those roof bits on, it'll collapse, you know."

Patty peered out from her makeshift walls, scowling.

"I thought you were too old to make dens," she retorted.

Nowadays, though, she kept hushing them angrily.

"I didn't notice what a racket you two make," she said, "not until Daddy came back. It jars with him, all this sniping at each other. And Patty, go and brush your hair. Your father will be home in less than half an hour."

Patty muttered that she'd never had to brush her hair during the day before.

Father picked up Patty when he came in, and he asked Audrey about school. They were both getting used to him, three weeks down the line.

"Smells good," he said. "When do we eat, Winny, my darling?"

"Audrey was supposed to clean the pan once Mum had made the mash," Patty said smugly, "but she said she was too busy. I had to do it."

Audrey turned on her. "Don't you dare. You're always making out you do more errands than me. Everyone knows the

"Audrey Bains!" Patty put her little hands on her hips. "Making things up as usual"

"I'm just trying to help," she said, but soon they were working together.

When Dad came back from visiting a friend in his regiment, he came out to the back and found them there. It became quite a project. They all got splinters, but the result, Dad said, would have impressed his Sergeant Major.

Audrey and Patty bickered like all sisters. Before the war, Mother had mainly ignored it.

"Go and do that upstairs, silly girls," she'd say. "I'm not interested."

older one does more, and you did not do the washing-up! Mum had virtually finished it when you –"

"Audrey Bains!" Patty put her little hands on her hips. "Making things up as usual. I'm going to tell Mum how you took a whole spoonful of sugar yesterday when there's hardly any –"

"It was not, not, not a whole spoonful. I already said you hardly know what a spoonful is."

"I do so. It's –"

"Be quiet!" Mum's voice was shrill, and

Continued overleaf

the two girls' mouths snapped shut. "How could you? How can you keep bickering, making a mess, and fighting over… over *sugar*, when we're all trying so hard to –"

"Don't try so hard, love." Charlie's voice was soft, but it cut straight through Winny's. He was smiling at the girls. "It's funny, you have to admit, them quarrelling over what a spoon is!"

Winny looked distressed.

"I just want this home to be a nice place for you, and it's hard, when –"

"Is it?" He stepped towards her and put his arms around her waist. "I like the noise, love, and I'm very happy with everything not being smart. I'm happy with mess, because it's my family's mess. Can you see that?"

She looked up at him. "It should be special, now you're home. I've been so looking forward."

"Oh, my Winny, so have I. To the mundane routine, and the children under my feet. Yes, even the bickering. It's a home, with real people in it, the people I love. It's what I dreamed of – and in my dreams nobody did their hair or ironed anyone's socks.

"Listen. When I lay awake at night in Italy, I'd imagine the four of us, sitting round the wireless with our shoes off and our cups of tea on the rug. True, I saw two fat little things running about, rather then these two young ladies, but the home of my daydreams was not perfect."

"Not like the newsreel?" Patty took her father's hand.

"What newsreel was that, sweetheart?" he asked, letting go of his wife and

bending down to be closer to Patty.

Audrey and Patty described the film.

He laughed. "We saw that too, or something like it, in a cinema on our way home, down in Kent. Goodness knows what made them show us that! My mate Colin, he said to me, 'I hope my Iris isn't wearing them silly shoes. We've a poultry business to run!' George said he didn't like the look of the two kids at all, shiny faces like Brylcreem. He said they looked like china dolls. He said his boy always has a big egg on his head from falling out of a tree, and quite right too!"

Mother looked at the floor. He went over and gently tilted up her chin so that she had to look at him.

"I don't want to live in a newsreel," he said. "I want to live here."

There was a pause. Then Winny smiled.

"We'd better take our shoes off, then," she said. "Dr Morelle's on in a minute, on the radio."

Patty threw herself at the wireless and switched it on to warm up.

"Shall I bring the last of the Dundee cake, to eat on our knees?" Audrey asked. "We did that before Dad came home."

"Oh, we did that, your mum and I, before you were a twinkle in anybody's eye," he said.

Then Winny kissed him.

"Welcome home, Charlie," she said.

THE AUTHOR SAYS…

"My great-uncle got out of a Japanese POW camp in 1946. He and his family had some adjusting to do – it was far from easy. His story sparked this one…"

Brain BOOSTERS

Missing Link

The answer to each clue is a word which has a link with each of the three words listed. This word may come at the end (eg **HEAD** linked with **BEACH, BIG, HAMMER**), at the beginning (eg **BLACK** linked with **BEAUTY, BOARD** and **JACK**) or a mixture of the two (eg **STONE** linked with **HAIL, LIME** and **WALL**).

ACROSS

1 Book, Out, Word (4)
3 Activity, Labour, Sciences (8)
8 Bridal, Driver, Express (5)
9 Autograph, Photograph, Record (5)
11 Box, Liquid, Ploughman's (5)
12 City, Triangle, Truths (7)
14 Euro, Film, Struck (4)
16 Butter, Coffee, Tea (4)
20 Moth, Penguin, Purple (7)
22 Nellie, Peach, Toast (5)
24 Fool, Reader, Shower (5)
26 Counter, Saxophone, Trombone (5)
27 Captive, Studio, Target (8)
28 Belt, Cushion, Window (4)

DOWN

1 Crossword, Jigsaw, Monkey (6)
2 Sheets, Stitch, Wood (5)
4 Bargain, Fortune, Gatherer (6)
5 Certificate, Holding, Plough (5)
6 Corn, Loaf, Nut (3)
7 Figure, Grand, Time (6)
10 Bottle, Round, Shake (4)
13 Afternoon, Cat, Kin (3)
15 Felt, Top, Wing (3)
16 Clean, Home, Second (6)
17 Freeze, Fry, Rooted (4)
18 Circle, Fox, Ocean (6)
19 Black, Flea, Place (6)
21 Air, Automatic, Range (5)
23 At, Print, Scale (5)
25 Boy, English, Flame (3)

Hidden word in the shaded squares:

Solutions on page 161

Back From Outer Space

When your entire world changes, you can find a whole new life in the most surprising small things…

By Susan Sarapuk

Look what I found in the garden, Mum," Harry held up a golf ball, wet from the dew-soaked grass.

We'd recently moved and our new house backed onto the golf course.

"Can I keep it?"

We should have tossed it back over the hedge really, but before I could suggest it Harry buried it in his jumper.

"Maybe it's come from outer space," he said. "Perhaps there's a secret code hidden inside it."

"It's a golf ball, Harry…"

"But perhaps there are little aliens inside. I'll put it somewhere safe."

Before I could say anything further he skipped off to his bedroom.

Harry has his obsessions. It all started after his dad left, and even though there was little I could do about it, I still feel partly responsible. He has no brother or sister to share this difficult time with; it's just him and me against the world and I guess he's created his own safe haven within that.

His toys have to be put back in the exact same spot, at mealtimes he lines up his cutlery meticulously, and as we walk down the garden path on the way to school every morning he avoids the cracks between the paving stones.

"Why?" I asked him one day.

"Because the world may end, Mum," came the answer. I felt even more guilty then because the world he once knew *had* already ended.

So if he wanted to pretend that there were aliens inside a golf ball that someone had thwacked into our garden I wasn't going to argue with him.

Harry wasn't settling in very well at school. He hadn't brought any new friends home and when I asked him if he'd made any he shrugged and said, "Justin let me play chess with him when it was raining lunchtime."

"Did you beat him?"

"Yeah."

Of course he did; Harry's clever. Sometimes I worry that he's too clever and won't fit in.

"But the others won't let me play football in the yard with them."

I had visions of poor Harry standing

Continued overleaf

on the sidelines longing to join in yet being excluded. I tried to remember what it was like being the new kid trying to break into established patterns, but I couldn't because I'd never been that person. Susie and I were friends from the first day we met and remained so throughout our schooldays.

However, like Harry, I was trying to cope with new things now.

"It's OK Mum," Harry said.

Nevertheless, I felt for him as he disappeared off to his room.

The following day Harry found another golf ball.

"It's another message from outer space," he said as he brought it inside from the garden.

"Maybe someone's looking for it," I said. "Go outside and look over the hedge and see."

"There's no-one there, Mum. The aliens sent it."

"Harry, it's a golf ball. Someone's hit it off the course and into our garden!" I sounded harsher than I meant to, but this

was a piece of paper filled with drawings and scribbles – I could decipher a picture of aliens with bug eyes and antennae sticking out of their over-large heads.

I didn't know whether to applaud his imagination or be worried. I'd pitched Harry into an alien world by taking him away from the place he'd grown up after his dad had already left him. Maybe this was his way of coping with it.

I deliberated whether to take the golf balls and throw them back over the hedge.

In the end I decided not to – they probably meant more to my son than any middle-aged golfer on the course who was probably well off enough to afford some new ones.

I picked up Harry's dirty clothes for the laundry and closed the bedroom door behind me.

I was hanging out the clothes on the line when I heard an intense rustling in the hedge, followed by an expletive. Then a head appeared over the hedge.

"Sorry, I didn't realise anyone was there. I lost my golf ball… not the world's greatest golfer."

I didn't know whether to applaud Harry's imagination or be worried about him

fixation was beginning to worry me.

"How do you know?" he challenged. "It could have dropped from the sky." He stormed off with his treasure.

After he'd left for school the following morning I went into his room to tidy up. The two golf balls sat side by side on his desk by the window. Alongside there

The voice belonged to a man in his forties, I would guess, with a friendly face and neat black hair.

"I'll see if it's in the garden," I pegged out the last of Harry's shirts and went to investigate.

"You're new," he said as I pushed my toes through the swathes of long grass. "I mean, I play regularly and this house has

"Someone was looking for a missing golf ball the other day," I told Harry.

"No Mum, the Andromedans are trying to communicate with us and they've chosen me."

"Harry!"

"I've got to work out what they're trying to say!"

Once again he rushed off before I could say anything further.

My concern was increasing; maybe I ought to speak to one of the teachers in school. I opened his bedroom door later to find him furiously scribbling, a row of golf balls on the desk in front of him.

"What are you writing Harry?" I asked tentatively.

"It's secret," he replied and covered his work with his arm.

"You know it's not real, don't you? They're just golf balls. They haven't come from outer space."

"You don't know anything, Mum!"

He turned his back to me and hunched over his work.

I looked up from cutting the grass as a voice shouted over the sound of the stuttering lawn mower. "Hello again!"

"Hello," I answered as I turned it off. "Have you lost another ball?"

"No, I just thought I'd say hello again," Tom smiled.

"You must have a good job if you can be out on the golf course so much." I made the comment then wished I hadn't.

"I'm a freelance writer," he explained. "I like to start the day with a round of golf a couple of times a week. I'm Tom Ryland by the way."

"I'm Jess Norton," I exchanged pleasantries. "Harry's found loads of golf

been empty for a while."

"We moved in a month ago; me and my son Harry."

"You might have found some more of my golf balls then," he joked. His smile lit up the morning. I didn't mention the couple Harry had found.

"Hey Tom!" came a cry from further along the hedge. "It's over here!"

"Found it. I'm trying to improve," he rolled his eyes and chuckled. Then he gave a wave and disappeared and I bent down to retrieve the laundry basket.

Mum, I've found some more golf balls!" Harry came racing in from the garden.

I wondered if they belonged to the mysterious Tom. How often did he play and how bad was he really?

Continued overleaf

balls in the garden – he thinks they've come from outer space." I don't know why I said that either; it made us sound mad.

"Great imagination the kid has!" Tom Ryland said.

I didn't say that I was scared it was so much more than that.

"Maybe I'll see you again," he waved and went back to his friends.

He did see me again. I don't know why, but I worked out the days he was playing and contrived to be doing something in the garden on those mornings.

The next time I went into Harry's room there was no sign of the golf balls and I heaved a sigh of relief.

"I see the golf balls have gone. Did you throw them back over the hedge?" I said over tea that evening.

"No, I put them in the drawer. I didn't want them sending out probes when I was trying to sleep. Aliens can fry your brain, you know."

I didn't point out that if there were truly aliens inside the golf balls then wrapping them up in underwear and putting them in a wooden drawer wasn't going to stop them sending out mind probes – then I gave a mental *aargh!* as I

I wasn't sure how Harry would deal with the news I was going on a date with Tom

The jungle soon became a well-tended plot, and Tom always halted his play to stop and say hello over the hedge.

"You should play," he said one day.

"I don't know how to," I confessed.

"You could always have lessons. And what about Harry? Would he like to learn how to play?"

It was a possibility. He still hadn't invited any friends around to our house and didn't say much about what was happening at school.

I told him about Tom's offer.

"Who is he?" he frowned.

"He's a writer. I told him about your golf balls and he thinks you've got a great imagination."

Harry chewed on that for a while before saying: "I haven't worked out what they're trying to tell me yet."

My heart sank once more.

realised what I was thinking. There are no aliens inside the golf balls!

"Harry," I said gently. "This is getting serious."

"Too right it is, Mum; they're planning to take over the world."

Our morning meetings were becoming a regular thing. I even heard Tom's companions joking one day: "Here we go, the ten minute break! I bet you're losing your golf ball on purpose."

One day I made a flask of coffee and invited them all to have a break over the hedge. Afterwards Tom's companions gave him a significant look and slunk off.

"What's up with them?" I frowned.

"Er, I don't really know you Jess… well, only what you've told me…"

"Likewise."

"There's a do at the clubhouse next

Friday and, er… I know you're not long separated but, um… would you like to come with me?"

I didn't even have to think before I said yes. Brian seemed a very long time ago and I suddenly realised that emotionally we'd left each other long before our official separation.

"Great," he gave a sigh of relief, then grinned. "Maybe then we can stop meeting over the hedge!"

I wasn't sure how Harry would deal with the news that I was going on a date with Tom; I didn't want to push him further over the edge into his aliens obsession. I pondered and fretted over it all day.

When he came home from school he was beaming.

"Guess what, Mum!"

I hadn't seen him so cheerful for a very long time.

"Everyone loves my stories!"

"What stories?" I asked.

"About the aliens. I started writing about them. Mrs Pugh read out one of my stories to the class. I've written loads so at lunchtime I started passing them out in the yard and everyone wants to read more. Everyone thinks I'm cool! And Jack and Liam and Peter want to come around to play tomorrow. Can they?"

"Of course they can!" A rush of relief engulfed me. "Tell them to come for tea."

Friends at last! I felt a weight lift from my shoulders.

Harry didn't mind about me going to the golf club with Tom, especially when Jack invited him for a sleepover that night. And when I said he could learn to play golf he was enthusiastic.

When I went into his room to place clean laundry in the chest of drawers I noticed the golf balls were gone.

"Harry, did you throw them back?" I asked him.

"No, Mum," he said. "Simon in school said you can get money for returning golf balls so I took them to the club yesterday and got five pounds!"

"Oh." It was on the tip of my tongue to make a comment about aliens but I bit it back. There was no need to. Harry had his new friends and new interests, and he didn't need them anymore. I thought of Tom and smiled – my universe was opening up as well; maybe I *had* found Andromeda in a golf ball, too.

THE AUTHOR SAYS…

"This quirky story just popped into my mind! My friend lives close to a golf course and regularly finds golf balls in the garden."

Man Of The Moment

It seems unthinkable – but will loyal Guy be tempted by the charms of a determined yummy mummy?

By Suzanna Ross

Archie screwed up his face as Guy covered it with a dollop of Factor 50.

"Why do I need that horrible stuff?"

It was clear the boy wasn't happy.

"Because your mother said so." Guy moved his attention to what was visible of small arms and legs.

"Where's Mummy, anyway? Why can't she come with us?"

"She's at work, Archie. You know that."

"But it's Saturday."

Guy sympathised with Archie's frown. Bernice was always at work these days.

He knew she bore the responsibility of being the breadwinner and he was grateful she was so successful, really he was. But that didn't stop him wishing she was here a bit more often.

"Come on then, young man." Guy popped a sunhat onto Archie's head. "Let's get going."

Quite apart from anything else, Guy reflected as they walked to the park, Bernice was missing out on so much. It seemed like only yesterday that Archie had been a baby and now, in a matter of days, he would be moving up from nursery to school.

At the park, Archie ran for the swings and Guy settled himself on a nearby bench. He sighed as he noticed Nicole making her way over.

"Morning," he said, barely looking up as she sat down. He didn't want to encourage her.

"Bernice working again this weekend?" Nicole asked.

Guy was silent. Even if he was unhappy, he wasn't about to be disloyal.

"Another woman will snap you up," Nicole continued. "If she's not careful."

Guy cringed. Nicole had made it clear more than once that she would be very happy to do any such snapping.

It pained him to admit, but maybe he should listen to what she had to say. He'd always love Bernice – and, of course, Archie – but he still had some pride. Staying where he wasn't needed wasn't his style.

"We're going to have this conversation soon. You know that as well as I do," she persisted.

He glanced meaningfully to where Archie and Nicole's children were playing in the sand pit.

"Not here. Not now," he told her urgently.

Continued overleaf

Continued from previous page

The last thing he needed was Archie telling his mother that Guy had been talking to this woman. He needed to be the one to tell Bernice.

"Sit down, Guy," Bernice said once Archie was in bed that evening.

She smiled as she handed him a glass of wine – a clear signal that he was off duty in terms of babysitting.

She must be staying in.

Quite unexpectedly, his heart skipped a beat. But then he realised what her request for a quiet chat must mean. Disappointment surged through him and settled somewhere in his boots.

Even though he'd known

"I'll need you more than ever – there will still be school runs, evenings I have to work, school holidays…"

He sighed. That wasn't exactly what he'd hoped to hear. But then she reached out and lightly touched his hand.

"I didn't even know how much you mean to me," she admitted, "until I realised I might lose you."

He could barely breathe.

"Nicole mentioned evenings off." His gaze didn't waver and he knew, as he looked into her eyes, that he hadn't been mistaken – Bernice felt the same way.

"Care to make a counter offer?" he murmured.

"How about evenings in? With me?"

"You're never home."

"We've had a difficult

"I didn't even know how much you mean to me until I realised I might lose you…"

for a while that his time with Bernice was coming to an end, he still wasn't ready to leave.

"I understand Nicole's been making advances." She took a large gulp of her own wine.

"How did you hear?"

"The grapevine." She grimaced. "I hope you don't think I'll be letting you go without a fight."

He raised an eyebrow and was fascinated to see a soft blush warm her cheeks.

"I haven't told you often, but I need you, Guy," she said, all big brown eyes.

"You won't when Archie goes to school," he pointed out.

time of it lately with the merger, but that's all over now – so I'll be home more."

Guy grinned – and, slowly, she relaxed and smiled back.

He'd been a little concerned when his mates had warned him, as a male nanny, he'd be an easy target for yummy mummies. But, as he leaned in for their first kiss, he had to admit that being Bernice's target had its appeal.

● ●

THE AUTHOR SAYS…

"These days it's nothing unusual for a mother to be the breadwinner. But it does mean someone needs to take responsibility for childcare."

Daisy Butter Shortbread

Ingredients (Makes 30)

- **Vegetable oil, for greasing**
- **225g butter, at room temperature, cut into pieces**
- **110g caster sugar**
- **350g plain flour**
- **Pinch of salt**

To decorate:

- **Pink ready-to-roll icing**
- **Tiny sugar flowers**

1 Preheat the oven to 180°C, Fan Oven 160°C, Gas Mark 4. Lightly grease three baking sheets with a little vegetable oil.

2 Put the butter into a large mixing bowl with the caster sugar. Beat with a wooden spoon until thoroughly incorporated – although it isn't necessary to beat until light and fluffy.

3 Sift in the flour and salt and work into the mixture with the wooden spoon, until it looks like crumbs. Gather the mixture together and form into a ball. Transfer to a lightly floured surface and knead lightly and quickly until smooth, but avoid too much handling.

4 Roll out the dough to a thickness of about 5mm. Cut out biscuits with a flower-shaped cutter, or stamp out circles using a 5cm biscuit cutter, re-rolling the dough as necessary. Carefully lift onto the baking sheets.

5 Bake for about 15min until light golden brown. Cool for a few minutes, then transfer to a wire rack to cool completely.

6 To decorate, roll out pink icing thinly and use a daisy cutter and stamp to cut out shapes. Dampen the undersides with a little water, then place on the biscuits, putting a sugar flower in the centre. Leave until set, then store in an airtight tin.

RECIPE AND FOOD STYLING: SUE ASHWORTH PHOTOGRAPHY: JONATHAN SHORT

The Last Witch

Hubble, bubble… oh, come on! Who really believes any of the old myths about wise women like me?

By Jan Snook

I t's not easy being a witch. Not these days, anyway. As far as I know, I'm the last one in Britain. There must be others around, but it's not something people advertise – they're frightened of being labelled nutters.

Oh dear, you've probably labelled me already. Honestly, I'm a nice, normal woman. Apart from being a witch.

I think my family survived because in the 1600s they moved to Wales. England

innocent? Lot of rubbish, obviously. No proper witch would have stuck around for such a primitive trial.

The thing is, they were almost right. If they'd put a real witch in water, and she'd stayed there for more than a minute or two, the water would have bubbled around her. We make water boil, I don't know why.

Doesn't do us any harm, but it's a bit of a nuisance. I can only swim if I'm sure there's no-one around. My mum had to tell the school I was allergic to chlorine when I was a child, to stop anyone finding out.

I've done a lot of good, and no-one's ever noticed if a little magic was tucked in

and Scotland tended to blame any bad luck on witches, and tried people left, right and centre. The Welsh put any mischief down to fairies, which let us off the hook.

Witchcraft was still a criminal offence in Britain till 1736. Imagine!

There's a funny thing about witches. You know how they used to dunk suspected witches in the village duck pond, and if they sank they were deemed

Anyway, I come from a long line of wise women, as witches used to be known. They were the midwives of the villages, which is why I'm a midwife.

Oh, there you go again, wondering why anyone like me would be allowed anywhere near the health service. Well, let me tell you, I've done a lot of good in my time, and no-one's ever noticed if there **Continued overleaf**

Continued from previous page

was maybe a little magic tucked in.

Of course, I've never married. I've had my chances – but you simply can't be married to someone for years and them never notice you're a witch.

Sometimes, even when I'm trying my very hardest, I've slipped up. Once, on a night out when I was a bit tipsy, I re-filled all the glasses at our table without bothering to go to the bar. Fortunately my friends were equally merry and didn't notice…

So no husband and no children, which is a pity. Delivering other women's babies is as close as I get.

Then, when I saw her today, she looked at me as if she recognised me.

The mother was full of anxious questions – typical first-time mum stuff. It's incredible how little they know. Not like the olden days, when everyone had big families and there was always a mother, older sister or aunt nearby.

The baby looked rather grubby, between you and me, so I offered to teach the mother how to bath her. I don't know why I said it, except for that odd look in the baby's eyes… Usually I avoid water like the plague.

Anyway, we went up to the bathroom and I issued the mother with instructions. She

Not only could this day-old baby focus, she looked at me as if she recognised me

I've just got in from doing a house visit, actually. A postnatal visit to a woman who gave birth yesterday.

She was booked in to the local maternity ward, but she didn't get there in time so I had to rush out to her. Odd, really. I had the impression she was desperate not to go to hospital.

Anyway, she had a lovely little girl, quite small, but masses of dark hair and amazing eyes. Her mother's eyes. They say babies can't focus, but this one could.

had all the paraphernalia new mothers seem to have these days, bath thermometers and the like, and she got the water to the right temperature and carefully lowered the child in. Most babies cry the first time they have a bath, but not this one. She lay there, cool as a cucumber, watching as the first few bubbles rose to the surface, and the water gradually reached simmering point.

Her mother and I looked at each other. The baby didn't even go pink.

THE AUTHOR SAYS…

"There have always been stories about witches, in every society and age. Perhaps we all have days when we'd like to think there was magic in the world!"

FANCY THAT!

Fascinating facts about **the world's forests**

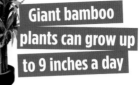

Giant bamboo plants can grow up to 9 inches a day

✦ The Guinness World Record for "World's Most Dangerous Tree" is held by the manchineel tree from the Gulf of Mexico. Its sap burns and blisters skin and can cause blindness if it gets in your eyes.

✦ **The Trembling Giant is a colony of quaking aspen trees in Utah. It's actually a single organism connected by one massive root system, and thought to be the oldest living organism at 80,000 years old.**

✦ Around 80% of the food we eat originally came from rain forests. Some popular ones include coffee, chocolate, rice, tomatoes, potatoes, bananas, black pepper, pineapples and corn.

✦ **80% of the flowers in the Australian rain forests are not found anywhere else in the world.**

A fully-grown oak in the UK grows – and sheds – 250,000 leaves every year and produces around 50,000 acorns in a good year

The Central African Forest has more than 8000 species of tree

✦ There are three main types of forest on the planet: tropical or rain forests (found near the equator), temperate forests, and boreal forests (found in colder climates).

✦ **The height above sea level at which trees cannot grow is called the tree line and changes with latitude. In the Alps it's around 7000ft, while in North Wales a mere 1820ft.**

✦ Tropical rain forests only cover about 6% of the Earth's surface, but are home to more than half the world's plant and animal species.

✦ Britain is thought to have the largest population of ancient trees in Europe.

✦ **The tallest tree in the world is a Coast Redwood called Hyperion growing in California's Redwood National Park. It stands at 380ft – taller than Big Ben and the Statue of Liberty.**

✦ Trees can talk to each other! When insect pests threaten willows, they emit a chemical warning to nearby trees, which secrete more tannin to put the invaders off.

Our Little Family

I was utterly crushed; our dreams weren't to be. But there was a helpless creature who needed us...

By Patsy Collins

While we were waiting to go in, Duncan held me close so my tears soaked his shirt and told me about a fox he'd seen at work.

"It was there a few days ago. Looked like it had been hit by a car or something. I considered trying to get it to a vet but it ran off before I could get near it, let alone think about catching it. It was dragging a leg but still moved faster than I can."

"Poor thing. I hope it didn't suffer long."

"Oh, it's not dead. I see it every morning and a few of us have started leaving behind any food we've got left. It's gone by morning so I suppose he eats it."

"And the leg?"

"Still dragging. I can't tell if it hurts him."

Then our names were called and I forgot all about the fox.

Duncan was upset too, I knew. He comforted me and continued to function normally but I knew he was disappointed.

No – more than that. In his way he, too, was grieving. We've been together since we were at school, you see, and we've been thinking about the family we'd raise since we were children ourselves.

Plenty of people told us our relationship wouldn't last and I think we believed them until we realised, at twenty-five, that we'd been together more than half our lives.

We got married the following year and those people who'd once said it wouldn't last started asking when we'd start a family. We laughed and said we'd hardly thought about it.

It wasn't true; we'd picked out names, lots of names. We were going to have eight children and give them so many

We've been thinking about our future family since we were children ourselves

The test results were a relief in a way. It meant we needn't go through any fertility treatments, fill in more charts, keep saying, "no, not yet" to our mothers.

I kept telling myself all that, whenever I wasn't sobbing so hard that I couldn't think at all.

names their initials spelled out words. We'd have all boys, or all girls. Half and half, twins, triplets. We'd refined our plans to just Emily and Jamie by the time we married. But that was our business. Something private.

Continued overleaf

Continued from previous page

That's what we thought at first, anyway. As the months without sign of a baby turned into years, it gradually seemed to be everybody's business.

Not any more, though.

After a time I got a grip on my grief. I don't mean it lessened, but I stopped crying all the time and began to give an impression of someone getting on with her life.

I got another picture of him today," Duncan said one evening.

"Who?"

"The fox."

I'd been so wrapped up in my misery, it took me a moment to understand what he was talking about. He'd probably been giving me regular updates on the poor creature but I'd not paid attention.

It wasn't fair for Duncan to lose his wife as well as the children he'd hoped for.

"Show me," I said encouragingly.

The picture on his phone wasn't very

but I could control some things about my future. I could consider fostering or adoption, I could decide to accept that we'd not have a family and decide to travel or… well, there were lots of options.

When I told Duncan, he was delighted I was feeling more positive and beginning to look forward. However he didn't do what I'd done – and what I'd expected from him – and seize on one of those options as the obvious answer.

"Adoption is something to think about," I prompted.

"I believe it's quite complicated, though, and a lot of people don't get selected." He squeezed my hand. "We can look into it, if you like."

Maybe it seems odd that we'd not considered adopting, but you don't if you're so sure you'll have your own child and I'd been sure for so long. I mean, I had realised that some people get pregnant the minute they come off the Pill and I hadn't, and that most people get pregnant

"Franz sits right under Dave's cab window and catches chips as he drops them"

clear as the fox was lurking in a shadow, and none too close, but I could see it was horribly thin.

"It's putting on weight, though, I'm sure. Here – look."

He scrolled through and showed me the first photo he'd taken. He was right, it had looked even worse before.

The next day I accepted the counselling I'd been offered. It helped a little. I was told about taking control of my situation. I couldn't change the fact that Duncan and I would never have a baby,

within a year of trying and I hadn't.

By two years Duncan and I had worked out there was a chance that something wasn't quite right but we just thought it was a delay, not a no.

I'd got on the internet and looked for things we could do. I learned the best time to conceive and about taking my temperature, hence the charts I no longer needed. We adopted a healthier diet, exercised more. Duncan got cool, roomy underwear. Oh and we did some weirder things too; we ate a lot of yams, took

phases of the moon into account and I spent a lot of time lying with my feet in the air after… you know, afterwards.

It was fun at first and there was no hurry. We'd been happy just the two of us for sixteen years, and we were still young. Another few months wouldn't matter.

Of course none of it helped, but that wasn't the fault of the world wide web. So I tried it again for my latest, far more minor problem; Duncan's fox. He'd told me it wasn't gaining any more weight.

"Everyone gives it scraps now and it's getting quite tame. I dropped the piece of pastry I was going to throw and he ran up and snatched it from right by my boot.

"And Dave, one of the lorry drivers, always brings him chips and Franz sits right under his cab window and catches them as they fall." He smiled.

"Franz?" I raised my eyebrows.

"A bit more classy than Freddie, I thought." He shrugged.

And why not? We'd decided on Emily for our imaginary daughter because he considered it a classier version of the name of our favourite Spice Girl.

"So he's eating well but not getting any better?"

"I think the leg is improving a bit, but he doesn't look healthy."

After we'd eaten, I looked up urban foxes on the internet. I read that a diet of scraps wasn't ideal for them. Obvious really, when you think about it.

"I think Franz needs to start a healthy eating plan," I declared. "Take him the mince that's sitting in the fridge."

"The best steak mince you were going **Continued overleaf**

to make me spaghetti Bolognese with?"

"I can buy more tomorrow so you'll still get your spaghetti. You're worried about him, aren't you?"

"Suppose. Do you think I'm silly?"

"No. Caring, that's what you are."

That's one of the reasons he'd make such a good dad, but I didn't say so then.

I waved him off the following morning, with his box of salad and pack of raw mince. Then I did the chores, including buying some offcuts of meat for Franz, before returning to the computer.

I typed "adoption" into the search engine. It took the seconds needed for the

him some of the things my internet searches had revealed.

He towelled his hair and said, "We need to think about it, look into things."

"I have," I started to say but then stopped. I had rather sprung it on him and Duncan is the sort who likes to think things through before making a decision. You know, date a girl for twelve years before proposing, that kind of thing.

I restrained my enthusiasm and tried to give him space by changing the subject.

"Did Franz enjoy his mince?"

"Seemed to. I sprinkled it over the grass so I could get another picture and he ate every scrap. Let me show you."

He'd taken several pictures of Franz

Apparently hiding the medication in a jam sandwich was the recommended option

first image of a woman with a baby in her arms to load for me to decide adoption was the answer.

Several hours of searching later, I was convinced we met all the criteria and had a good chance of adopting a baby; an even better chance if we agreed to take a slightly older child. That was my favoured option as it would make up for some of the time we'd lost.

I downloaded all the information we'd need to start the process and waited for Duncan to come home.

"We can adopt," I blurted out before he'd got out the car. "I'm sure they'll accept us. I've got all the forms and everything."

"Whoa, calm down, love!"

"Sorry, I'm just excited."

"Yes – I can see that."

As he got washed and changed I told

and it was clear Duncan had got very close to the animal. It was clear, too, that Franz wasn't at all well. When I'd looked up urban foxes the day before, I'd seen photos of some suffering from mange and he looked just the same. I fired up the laptop to check the symptoms.

"Does he scratch himself?" I asked.

"Yes, he's always doing it."

"And you say he seems less frightened of you?"

"Yes. What are you looking at?" He read the page. "Yeah, I'm pretty sure that's what's wrong. Click that link, will you, the one for treatment."

We found that treatment was fairly simple if you could persuade the fox to swallow the medication and that he was likely to die slowly and painfully without it. There was no option; we ordered the cure

and read up on how to administer it. Apparently hiding it in a jam sandwich was the recommended option.

"Well he's going to eat healthily until the stuff arrives," I said as I put all my print-outs on adoption into a folder. I made sure my husband saw where I put it so he could look through when he was ready.

Duncan took meat to Franz for the rest of the week. We talked about the fox in detail and skirted around the subject of adoption.

"How can people give up a child?" he asked once.

"Lots of reasons." I gave a few examples.

"If we took a child, would we know why it had been abandoned?"

"I don't know, but does it matter?"

"How can we care for them if we don't know? What would we tell them?"

"I don't know, love, but we'd find a way. You don't know why there's a lame fox living in a car park in the middle of a city but you're doing your best to help him."

"I suppose."

When Franz's treatment arrived Duncan took jam sandwiches and meat for a while. The results were incredible. Duncan said the scratching stopped very quickly and Franz soon looked more alert, more like a wild creature than a sick and injured pet. Soon I could see the difference in the photos. Every time Franz looked better – though it got harder to tell as he no longer approached quite so close.

"I'm going to get some printed out," he told me. "Before and after kind of thing."

He did just that in his lunch break the following day. It was amazing to see the transformation Franz had gone through.

"Makes me feel quite proud to see what we've done."

"You did it," I told him.

"No, love. *We* did. We make a good team. I'll put these away now." He went to the drawer and took out my adoption file. "In here?"

Did that mean he was thinking he could show them to our adopted child one day?

"If there's room."

"There will be, once we've sent these forms off," he said.

It did mean that. I cried again.

Duncan, still holding the photos of the fox, held me close.

THE AUTHOR SAYS...

"I was writing in a building site car park (my life's like that). A fox appeared and was fed by several of the drivers. It clearly knew which lorries to approach."

Firework Night

In spite of having her own baby to care for now, our favourite feisty midwife is in the thick of it again!

By Catriona McCuaig

Maudie Bryant moved uneasily in her bed, wondering if she'd really heard a sound coming from downstairs, or was it a dream?

Her two-year-old son had resisted sleep until well past his usual bedtime, demanding drinks of water and arrowroot biscuits in an effort to put off the evil moment. She'd read his favourite book three times, and sung *The Runaway Train* until she was hoarse.

When at last he'd dropped off, she'd locked up for the night and turned in. Now something else had brought her back to consciousness.

She turned over, willing herself to fall back to sleep. Her years as a midwife had trained her to snatch sleep whenever and wherever she could, an invaluable skill when you had a toddler to bring up. But wait! There it was again. A soft whine, which meant that Rover was on the alert.

It was probably nothing more than a passing cat that has attracted his attention, yet she felt a frisson of alarm. Her husband, DS Dick Bryant, was at a police conference in Cardiff and she missed his comforting presence. She had never before feared being alone at night but now, when she was the sole protector of her little son, she felt differently.

Rover gave a sharp yelp. Maudie knew that sound. In a matter of minutes it would escalate into full-blown barking, and Charlie would be shocked awake to join the chorus.

Muttering to herself she fumbled for her slippers and made her way downstairs. She found the dog dancing beside the kitchen door, wide-eyed, with the fur standing up on his neck.

"I suppose we'd better go and have a look," she sighed, struggling to fasten the lead to his collar as he leapt for the door latch. "Just hang on while I find a torch!"

When she got the door open the dog almost dragged her off her feet in his eagerness, but fortunately his interest only led him to the nearby coal shed.

She had cursed that tumbledown building many times. Other people had coal sheds attached to their homes, or a coal chute leading into a cellar. Only the Bryants had to cross the yard in bad weather when they needed to fill the scuttle.

"Quiet, boy! You'll wake all the neighbours!"

Continued overleaf

Rover hurled himself against the door in a frenzy of excitement. Maudie lifted the latch, stepping back hastily in case a stray cat came shooting out.

Nothing moved. Rover moaned.

"Alright, boy! I suppose we'd better take a look. I only hope it's not some poor cat giving birth in there. The last thing I need is a litter of kittens!"

The dog was shivering now. Maudie shone her torch around, giving a nervous jump when the weak glow illuminated a crumpled pile of clothing in the corner. She gave a sigh of relief.

"It's alright, old boy. It's just a guy. Some of the local kiddies must have put it

delighted with the coloured lights? Was he too young for a packet of sparklers?

With that thought in mind, she fell asleep.

Rover was still agitated next morning and when she let him out he went straight to the coal shed, growling.

"I'll let you have a sniff," she told him, "Then perhaps you'll be satisfied!" But when she opened the door he crept away with his tail between his legs.

It was then she realised that she was seeing not a guy, but a very dead body!

"You've done it again, Mrs Bryant," Inspector Goodwood said when police officers were on the scene. "I trust you'll leave the investigating to us this time."

Perhaps the killer wanted the victim found, and so left the body in a policeman's shed?

there for safe-keeping. Little rascals! They might have asked me first."

She returned to the house, dragging the unwilling Rover behind her.

Bonfire Night was coming up, and every time she stepped outside the door she was accosted by children displaying an effigy of Guy Fawkes.

"Penny for the guy, Miss!" was their never-ending cry. The money they collected was used to buy fireworks, and for the children's sake she was glad to see the old customs being revived after the restrictions of the recent war years.

Rover would be driven mad by the loud noise of rockets and bangers on November the Fifth and she must remember to shut him indoors before the festivities started. Would Charlie be upset by the commotion, or would he be

Maudie nodded. It was hardly her fault that murder seemed to follow her around! She had promised Dick she would give up meddling in police affairs, and this time she meant it. She had been the prime suspect in a recent case; not an experience she wished to repeat.

Minding her own business was one thing; trying to forget about her gruesome discovery was quite another. Disjointed thoughts swirled around in her brain like angry midges before a thunderstorm. She tried to explain them to her friend Joan Blunt, the vicar's wife.

"I haven't a clue who the poor man was, but I'd like to know who put him in my coal shed," she said.

"The murderer, surely?"

"Yes, but why? And how did they transport him from wherever he was

killed? I didn't hear a vehicle during the night. Rover woke me with his whining but he didn't bark, as he always does if a car stops here."

"Perhaps the killer wanted his victim to be found quickly, so he left the body here knowing that Dick is a police detective," Mrs Blunt suggested.

"Oh, very considerate of him, I'm sure! And how would they have known that our shed was empty? For all anyone knew, it might have been full of old furniture!"

"It's a mystery to me, and no mistake."

On her way to the village shop Maudie encountered a group of small boys, jostling and shrieking in mock fury. They stopped fighting as she approached.

"Penny for the guy, missus?"

"Come off it, boys! You don't even have a guy with you. You can't expect me to fork out for nothing."

"Somebody stole our bogie, didn't they? How are we supposed to take a guy around without a bogie?"

Maude remembered seeing them going around the village with the chassis of an old pram, pulled by a length of old rope.

"I expect it will turn up somewhere," she told them. "But didn't I give you sixpence last week? Don't let me catch you trying to chisel money out of me again!"

As she continued on her way, the facts began to click into place. In the early hours of the morning she'd thought she was seeing an effigy of Guy Fawkes. Now the boys' bogie was missing. Who would want to steal part of an ancient pram unless it was to move something from

Continued overleaf

place to place? Such a person might be a neighbour of the young owner. If she knew who the boy was, it might provide a valuable clue. Quickly turning the push chair around, causing Charlie to gurgle with delight, she hurried back the way she had come, but the boys had disappeared.

When Dick telephoned from Cardiff that night she told him her suspicions.

"They've identified the victim," he told her. "His name is Josh Palmer. He was a dustman by trade, employed by the council in Midvale. I'll pass your information on to the boss, such as it is, but remember, old girl, don't meddle!"

"Of course not, dear," Maudie said, crossing her fingers as she hung up the receiver. Josh Palmer! That name rang a bell! *Wasn't that the man who…?*

Her mind went back to some visitors she'd received some weeks before. She'd answered the door to a grim-faced woman and a sullen teenager who had come to consult her professionally.

"My girl is in trouble," the woman said when they were in Maudie's kitchen, sipping cups of tea. "We want you to deliver the baby when her time comes and then see about getting it adopted."

"I'd like to help," Maudie said, "but I'm afraid I'm not practising just now. I have a baby of my own to look after, you see. You should speak to Nurse Baxter; she'll be able to help you."

"We don't want nobody knowing about Melanie's disgrace. We thought you could come to the house on the quiet, like."

Knowing how quickly gossip spread in the little village Maudie doubted that Melanie could keep her condition secret for very long. Did her mother propose to keep her locked in her bedroom for the last four months of her pregnancy?

"What about the father?" she suggested. "Is there any chance he'll marry you, Melanie?"

The girl shook her head.

"He says I can't pin it on him. He says the baby could be anybody's, but that's a lie, Nurse! I'm a good girl, I am. I've never been with nobody else, I swear!"

"He's scum, he is!" her mother snapped. "I'd never allow a daughter of mine to wed that Josh Palmer, even to give the baby a name!"

It was the old, old story, Maudie reflected. Melanie and her chap had attended the council school at the same time, although the boy was several years her senior. He had probably taken advantage of her youth and inexperience and now, when the inheritable had

happened, he was unwilling to take responsibility. Wishing the two women well, she had sent them on their way and had not heard from them since.

Now she went to the phone to tell Inspector Goodman what she knew.

In due course Dick reported that Paul Beacon, Melanie's father, had confessed to the crime. "He swears it was an accident, so they may be able to enter a plea of

mind that. If you don't need my professional help, what brings you here?"

"It's Dad! You've got to help me get him out of prison!"

Maudie frowned.

"I'm sorry, there's nothing I can do to help. As I understand it he's being kept in custody until his trial comes up."

"But I'm afraid they'll hang him, and he didn't do nothing!"

"They've identified the victim," Dick told Maudie when he phoned her that night

manslaughter. He only meant to give the chap a thrashing, and one can hardly blame him, what with his daughter in that condition. He used their Jimmy's bogie to take the body away."

"But why us?" Maudie asked. "Why bring the body here instead of dumping it in the woods, or something?"

"He says he couldn't think what else to do on the spur of the moment. He's the chap who brings our coal, Maudie. He hasn't made a delivery recently so he knew our shed would be near empty."

"It's easy when you know the answer," Maudie said, somewhat disappointed with this simple solution.

Two days later, she opened her front door to reveal a noticeably pregnant Melanie Beacon.

"You're not in labour, I hope," she told the girl, seeing the tears seeping down the swollen cheeks.

"What? No, Miss, I don't think so. How will I know when I am? I've asked Mum but she won't tell me nothing."

"Believe me, you'll know! But never

"Well, hardly nothing. Hasn't he confessed to killing your Josh?"

"He's not my Josh!" the girl shouted. "Mum's right. He was a no-good rat and I'm glad he's dead, so there!"

Maudie looked at the girl's contorted face. "It was you, wasn't it?" she guessed. "You killed Palmer and your Dad took the rap for you."

The girl nodded.

"Mum said it was best, only I can't let them hang him, Nurse, don't you see?"

"Of course you can't," Maudie said gently. "What really happened, Melanie? You can tell me."

"He came to the house, Josh did. He wouldn't marry me, but he wanted us to carry on like before. He said it didn't matter now on account of I was already in the family way. He made a grab for me and I tried to push him off. I must have caught him off balance because down he went. He hit his head on the fender and he went still. I thought he was shamming, waiting for me to bend down to see what happened so he could grab me, but I

Continued overleaf

Continued from previous page

waited and waited and he never got up. After that I fetched Dad, and Mum helped him load the body on our Jimmy's bogie."

"How did you know that Josh was actually dead?"

Melanie shrugged. "Dad thought he might still be breathing, but how was he supposed to know? He's not a doctor."

"If you'd called for help, the man might still be alive."

"There's no point trying to save vermin, Dad said. What will happen now, Miss? Will they hang me instead of Dad?"

"I shouldn't think so, dear. They don't

The general opinion in the village was that he had got what was coming to him

hang expectant mothers. You've done the right thing by coming to me. I'll just put in a call to the Midvale police station and we'll let the authorities take it from there."

Much later, Dick filled in the gaps. The medical evidence confirmed that Palmer had died as a result of a blow to the temple, inflicted when he fell across the fender. The coal man was charged with a variety of offences, including concealment of a dead body and making a false statement. For those crimes he would have to serve time.

The general opinion in the village was that Palmer had got what was coming to him; it later transpired that he had previously got two other young women into trouble, abandoning them without a shred of remorse.

"So that's that," Maudie said, with satisfaction.

"Yes, but I've said it before and I'll say it again, my girl," Dick countered. "You simply must stop interfering in police business. It's not safe and it's not right!"

She grinned at him. "Can I help it if people tell me things? Where's the crime in being a good listener? That's what nursing is all about."

"Nursing, my foot! They tell you things because you're known to be a meddler. Now, promise me you'll never interfere in a criminal investigation again."

"Yes, dear," Maudie vowed, crossing her fingers behind her back.

POCKET NOVELS!

Midwife Maudie appears in our series of romances – on sale in supermarkets and newsagents.

Brain BOOSTERS

Missing Link

The answer to each clue has a link with each of the three words listed. This word may come at the end (eg **HEAD** linked with **BEACH, BIG, HAMMER**), at the beginning (eg **BLACK** linked with **BEAUTY, BOARD** and **JACK**) or a mixture of the two (eg **STONE** linked with **HAIL, LIME** and **WALL**). Then find the shaded word.

ACROSS

1 Flower, Paper, Street (4)
3 Dive, Tail, Up (7)
8 Colour, Fresh, Mark (5)
9 Box, Mail, Speaking (5)
10 Glove, School, Whizz (3)
12 Chocolate, Clothes, Song (5)
14 Day, Fast, Lucky (5)
16 Button, Dancer, Flop (5)
20 Food, Reaction, Saw (5)
22 Above, Below, Boiled (3)
24 Escape, Finder, Scenic (5)
25 Clove, Hiker, Technical (5)
27 Cigarette, Fire, Fuel (7)
28 Beetle, Hunt, Night (4)

DOWN

1 Malt, Rye, Sour (6)
2 Key, Profile, Tide (3)
3 Drama, Killer, Number (6)
4 Booking, Guard, Warning (7)
5 Cloth, Sir, Tender (4)
6 Cart, Free, Wagon (6)
7 Brother, Ladder, Side (4)
11 After, Ages, Horse (4)
13 Hands, Thunder, Trap (4)
15 History, Monument, World (7)
17 Beer, Organ, Roll (6)
18 Automatic, Dish, Pressure (6)
19 Deep, Dry, Pan (6)
21 Bank, Book, Paper (4)
23 Aqua, Capacity, Iron (4)
26 Dog, House, Red (3)

Solutions on page 125

Cold Mountain

A terrible accident made Mac cut himself off. Could a guileless girl and an aimless youth open his heart?

By Paula Williams

As shoplifters went, the kid wasn't even very good. Drawing attention to himself with each furtive glance. The idiot might as well be wearing a striped jumper, black mask and carrying a bag marked "swag".

Mac took a jumper off the hanger. It was a horrible mustard-yellow, hand-knitted thing, which was probably why it ended up in a charity shop. Not that he gave a toss what it looked like. The people he mixed with didn't set too much store on sartorial elegance any more than he did. It was warm. It was cheap. Job done.

He turned to take it to the till. The kid was still by the CDs. Probably just browsing, after all. Whatever. None of his business.

The kid's head suddenly shot up as three lads of about the same age as him came up to the window. One signalled him to hurry up. Mac watched as the boy slipped the CD into his pocket and hurried out to his giggling mates. He saw him show them what he'd got, heard the shrieks of derisive laughter.

He saw, too, the kid's head go down, shoulders hunched, as he shoved the CD back in his pocket.

Mac shrugged. No need to get involved. He'd be moving on tomorrow. To another dead-end job in another dead-end town. At least this time accommodation of a sort went with the job. That would be good.

The nights were getting too cold to spend many more on the streets and the pain in his leg was getting worse the colder it got. Sleeping rough was not one of his better ideas.

The girl at the till looked ridiculously young to be alone in charge of a shop. No wonder the kids were stealing from her. Mind you, if she kept the more valuable items – like that little egg cup he was

Continued overleaf

The girl at the till looked ridiculously young to be left alone in charge of a shop

pretty sure was silver – nearer the till, that would be a start.

"I'm so glad someone's bought this." She smiled as she folded the jumper. "My gran knitted it for my brother and he refuses to wear it."

"Lucky for him he can afford to be choosy," Mac growled – and instantly regretted it. It came across as whingey and self-pitying and he was neither.

"Oh Lord, I'm so sorry." A flush stained the girl's pale cheeks. "I didn't mean to offend you."

"You didn't," he said tersely. Why didn't she just bag the thing and let him go? He didn't come in here to get her life history. Didn't want to know about knitting grannies. Certainly didn't want to think about his own, who didn't knit but worried. Even though he was thirty-two next birthday, she still worried about him. Probably a little less, to be fair, now that he'd given up climbing.

"I don't usually work in the shop," the girl was saying. "I'm happier looking after the animals, but the rescue centre needs

"No thanks." Mac grabbed the bag and headed for the door. What? Did she think he was a bloody charity case? Or maybe she thought he was the one who'd been nicking her precious biscuits.

He might look a down-and-out. He might shop in charity shops, but that didn't mean –

He stopped. He was angry. Hell, yes, he was angry. It was the first time he'd felt anything except an icy numbness since The Accident.

Correction. Since the day after, when Mrs Pearce had screamed at him, called him a murderer, said she hoped the knowledge that he'd killed her daughter would haunt him for the rest of his life. Well, she wasn't wrong there.

He'd coped by training himself to feel nothing. No pleasure. No joy at the sight of a sunrise, no warmth in the company of friends, nor even the comfort of a soft bed.

It was, he reckoned, a price worth paying. To be where no-one knew him, or tried to make him feel better by saying the

Mrs Pearce had called him a murderer. She hoped her girl's death would haunt him

the money desperately and when we had the chance of this empty shop for a few months, we jumped at it. I'm not very good at it, as you can probably tell.

"Take these biscuits, for example. There were eight of them but now there are only six and I know I haven't sold any. Look, I'm going to have a cup of tea and a biscuit while they're still here. Would you like one? I made them, so it's OK."

accident wasn't his fault. That he'd done all he could. He knew, just as Mrs Pearce did, that he hadn't.

Why then, had he got so angry, because a young woman with big, soft eyes and a sweet smile had offered him kindness? Was it because she'd seen him as an object of pity? Someone who couldn't even afford the price of a cup of tea and a biscuit? Who relied on the

"Look, I'm sorry, mate," Mac said loudly. "It's no good asking me about volunteering. You should ask the lady over there. It's her shop. I'm sure she can do with some extra help. Isn't that right?" he said as the smiley girl came across to them. "Who knows? She may even offer you a cup of tea and a biscuit while she tells you all about the rescue centre."

She looked surprised. Saw, too, the egg cup, upside down on the shelf. He could see she understood what had happened.

Would she call the police? Up to her. It was stupid of him to have got involved. It was just that there was something about the kid. He'd seen it many times before.

kindness of strangers? Much better to save her pity for the downtrodden donkeys and abandoned dogs.

As he reached the door, he was surprised to see the young shoplifter approaching and stood back to let him in. Then, on an impulse, he turned and followed him back into the shop.

Outside, the others were urging the kid on. Obviously, the CD was not to their taste; they'd sent him back for bigger fry.

The kid reached into his pocket, took out the CD and put it back on the shelf. Mac watched as he edged up to the shelf where the silver egg cup was. Saw the furtive look as he picked it up, the relief when he saw the girl was busy on the other side of the shop.

Without realising he was going to do it, Mac walked across and put his hand over the boy's stick-thin wrist, waited until the hand opened and the boy let the egg-cup go. He looked up at Mac, his eyes wide with fear.

Back in the day, before The Accident, he'd worked with kids just like him. Not bad kids, most of them. They came to the outdoor pursuits centre where he'd worked, full of bluster and bravado when they first got there. Scared witless at their first sight of a mountain close up, but trying desperately not to show it.

He used to get such a kick out of the ones who "got it", the ones who scraped their knuckles, cramped their leg muscles, forced themselves so far out of their comfort zones they'd never be the same again. The ones who stood with him on the top of the mountain, their eyes full of awe, their faces full of wonder.

This boy wasn't a bad kid, he just had some bad mates. Not that Mac gave a toss what happened to him, of course.

"Here," the girl gave the boy a beaming smile and handed him a leaflet. "It's really good of you to enquire about volunteering. We run the rescue centre on a shoestring, you know, and need all the

Continued overleaf

Continued from previous page

help we can get. Why don't you read that and, if you're still interested, come up to the centre, meet the animals, and we'll talk about it?"

The boy mumbled something barely audible and scuttled out of the shop.

"Thank you, Mac," the girl said quietly. "You handled that really well."

He spun round, his mouth dry.

"You know me?" he whispered, rubbing his hand through his straggling beard, his long, lank hair.

"I do now. You're Rob McKinley, aren't you? I wasn't sure when you first came in, but my brother – the one who hasn't the wit to recognise a good jumper when he sees one – he has a poster of you on his wall. Climbing's his passion, you see. You're one of his heroes."

Hero? He was no bloody hero. He was the guy who hadn't been able to stop a young girl fooling around on a mountain. Hadn't insisted she stayed with the group and not forge on ahead. Hadn't been able to get down to her quickly enough.

Hadn't been able to stop his own out-of-control tumble down the treacherous scree-covered slope as he tried to reach her, his leg snapping like a twig during the fall. Hadn't been able to move her, nor force her to hang on to life as they'd waited for the rescue party.

Had cradled her lifeless body, long after she'd gone.

"I was so sorry to hear about your accident," the girl said softly. "Sorry, too, about the girl. It wasn't…"

Mac's hands were shaking as he wrenched open the shop door. Time to move on. Fast. Before she had chance to tell him the accident wasn't his fault, that he was – what had they said at the enquiry that had exonerated him? – a hero.

So he did what all "heroes" do when they come up against something they can't handle. He ran – as fast as his wreck of a leg would carry him.

T hank you," Mac said as the man dropped money into the bowl. He felt a cold nose touch the back of his hand and reached to fondle the dog's head. Archie was never far from his side.

"Well, how are we doing?" Beth asked.

"The money's rolling in," Mac said. "It's typical of Tom to turn his leaving do into a fund-raising bash, isn't it?"

"He's a great kid, isn't he? And he's going to be a great vet, too."

"Yet look where volunteering's taken him," she said. "I knew from the first moment he turned up at the rescue centre he was as nuts about animals as I am."

"Nuts being the right word." Mac ducked quickly. Beth could pack a hefty punch – a result, she claimed, of standing up for herself against her bully of a brother. Her brother, now Mac's best friend, climbing partner, and soon-to-be best man at their wedding.

"Well, get on with it," Beth said. "There's a load of people heading this way who haven't bought raffle tickets yet. You're slipping."

Mac smiled as he watched her hurry

She brought him back, made him sit and listen and eat the awful biscuits she'd made

"He's got a long, hard slog ahead, though. Getting into vet school's one thing, staying there's another."

"He'll be absolutely fine, Mac. Don't be such a pessimist."

He pulled her towards him and kissed the top of her head. "You always see the best in everyone and I love you for it."

He loved her for a whole load of other things as well and there wasn't a day went by that he wasn't thankful for the way she'd run after him that day. Taken him back to the shop, made him sit and listen and eat those awful biscuits she'd made.

"Of course I see the best in people," she said. "And you don't, I suppose? That day in the shop, you could have had Tom arrested for shoplifting."

"And so could you," he pointed out. "You knew as well as I did he wasn't in the shop to volunteer."

away to talk yet more people into sponsoring donkeys or adopting ducks.

Beth could never resist a stray. She treated the frightened, the abused and abandoned with the same quiet patience she'd dealt with him. Gently, but firmly, she'd chased away his demons and dragged him back to life.

A life which, amazingly, she wanted to share. Along with four donkeys, a foul-mouthed parrot and goodness knows how many dogs, cats, chickens and ducks.

• •

THE AUTHOR SAYS...

"I am in awe of climbers. Combine that with those unsung heroes and heroines who give up their precious time to work in rescue centres and charity shops, and the result is a story that was a joy to write."

Little Mouse

Could Catherine endure a marriage of convenience to the intimidating and handsome Lord Tenby?

By Faye Scrivener

C atherine laid one hand on the damp-stained stone wall as she climbed the spiral stair to her chamber. Holding her skirts high with her other hand; she shivered as the chill of the night air radiated from the stones.

The day was almost spent and Catherine could barely see to put one foot in front of the other. The faint sound of the men's voices followed her up the stair and she was thankful that she had been allowed to leave the feasting in the great hall of the castle.

"My Lady." Catherine's own young maid, Mary, came scurrying out of a corner of the chamber. "Has the feasting ended?"

"Nay, Mary," replied Catherine. "But my head aches so, that His Lordship has allowed me to retire."

Mary hurried to assist her mistress in divesting herself of her corset and heavy skirts. The tiny jewelled head-dress was the final piece of her clothing to be removed. At last Catherine was comfortably attired in her long white night-gown. She sat by the hastily lit fire, while Mary heated some wine and herbs.

Sitting in the warmth and sipping the soothing posset, Catherine began to feel a little better. "Brush my hair, would you, Mary?" she asked, and began to relax even more as the child did as she was bid.

"Your hair is lovely, Madam," said Mary, as she took the brush slowly down the long tresses.

"Ah, if only that were true," replied Catherine. At eighteen years of age, she had shed the illusions of childhood. She knew that her hair at its best was of no particular merit. Its length was its only beauty, long enough that she could sit on it. But the colour was plain, neither fair nor dark but somewhere in-between, like the colour of a mouse. She was not ugly, she knew that from her mother's looking glass, but neither was she a beauty.

Continued overleaf

"They say the new queen has hair like yours," continued Mary, "but black as a raven's wing."

Catherine laughed; thinking of the sixth finger also rumoured to adorn the hand of the new queen. "They say a lot of things, Mary," she replied. "But who's to know the truth of it without going to Court to see for oneself?"

Her mind, slipped back to her mother's sunroom in those far off days, before she had become a wife.

"It is a good marriage, daughter," her mother had told her. "It will bring great advantage to our family. Lord Tenby is rich, by any standards, and not that old either. He may even present you to the King at Court one day, as long as you learn to control your temper."

Catherine bowed her head, pretending an obedience that she was far from feeling. "As you and my father see fit, mother."

The older woman laughed. "Don't play act with me, Catherine, I know you too well. But you will marry Lord Tenby, as long as he is willing once he has met you."

caught. "Handsome, mother?" she asked.

"Aye, and rich." Catherine's mother stroked her hair, a rare gesture of affection. "It will be well, child," she said.

A chill zephyr flew around the room, bringing Catherine back to the present, and the reality of her situation. *Rich*, she thought and smiled. The old draughty castle was hardly her idea of luxurious living and she was as far away from the glittering Court as it was possible to be. She sighed, and Mary redoubled her efforts with the brush.

"Enough, Mary," Catherine said, at last and bid the maid light the candles. At least they had candles, thought Catherine and not the cheaper rush lights as in the hall. Once she had learnt what was expected of her as the Lord's new bride, she would begin to make her presence felt here.

There would be small ways in which she could assert herself. Candles, for one thing, would be more plentiful and she would have the chimneys all swept. Much of the smoke from the fire was coming back into the room.

"It is a woman's lot to marry and have children. If fortunate, you might even be happy"

"I will endeavour not to discourage him," promised Catherine, who knew how important this match was to her family.

"It is a woman's lot in life to marry and have children," said her mother. "If you are fortunate, you might even be happy. They say he is handsome too, Catherine," she continued. "Almost," she dropped her voice to a whisper, "as handsome as the King himself."

Catherine looked up, her interest at last

At least her family had been right about one thing, Charles, Lord Tenby, was indeed handsome, if a little fearsome looking. When she had first risen from her deep curtsy on meeting him she had been taken aback by his red-gold beauty. He could indeed have been taken for a young relative of the King, had it not been dangerous for any to remark upon it.

"Greetings, my little mouse," he had said, lifting her to her feet. She had looked then into his eyes, and seen herself for what she was; a little mouse, plain and unnoticeable. At her age, she was lucky to have found a husband at all, she knew, and to be wed to this glorious creature was the stuff of dreams. She found herself wondering what magic it took to enthral such a man.

The wedding had been hurried and brief. Charles, though kind enough, was obviously not interested in his bride, hurrying from her presence whenever possible.

Whatever Catherine would have wished, she knew that the marriage was simply one of convenience for both families, though she knew nothing of the politics involved. Her father had deemed it a desirable match, and that was an end to it. In fact Catherine had already been promised, at birth, to a young French nobleman. That groom had died in a hunting accident before they could be married and a replacement had taken some time to find.

At last Lord Tenby was deemed to be a suitable match and Catherine knew she should be grateful. Her father had almost tarried too long in selecting a husband for her. She could not hope for more than a home and possibly a child every year.

Catherine had spent her life biting back any harsh words of defiance that would have provoked severe punishment. She had tried to control her temper as was becoming in a girl, but the household knew her as a sharp-tongued young lady.

Mindful of her good fortune she had made up her mind to be as sweet as honey to her new husband, in case he had been listening to the servants' gossip. Even though he obviously did not care for

her, she couldn't help but be pleased she had not been passed off to some old noble with rickety bones, and trembling, grasping fingers. She might not have managed to be so docile under that yoke.

As the night drew on, Catherine dismissed Mary and laid herself on the great four poster bed that dominated the chamber. The sound of laughter came towards her up the stair. Her husband was coming up to her chamber.

She shivered a little despite the warmth of the heavy wool coverlet. This was not their first night together, and Catherine had no fears on that score. She simply found the man's good looks intimidating and his avoidance of her gaze infuriating.

At last he staggered into the room. His face was suffused with colour and his eyes looked to be having trouble locating her.

"I am not that small a mouse, Sir," she said, "that you cannot find me in your bed." She spoke with her first show of anger since her arrival at the castle.

Charles laughed, the sound booming against the stone walls. "At last, my Catherine," he said, "the Lady reveals her true nature. No mouse here, I see." He staggered towards her.

"You are drunk, I believe, Sir," she said pushing herself away from him.

He laughed again. "Indeed so, Madam," he said and collapsed on the bed waving his feet. "Boots, I pray you."

"I shall call your man," said Catherine, gathering the bed sheets around her body. *I am no man's servant*, she thought, tears pricking at her eyes as she realised that

Continued overleaf

Continued from previous page

that was exactly what she was. She glanced back at her husband, still boot-waving on the bed and relented.

The boots came off with some difficulty, and Catherine was surprised at a sudden feeling of tenderness that overcame her as she beheld her lord's surprisingly small feet. "You should have removed your boots after the hunt, My Lord," she said with a sniff.

Charles lurched into a sitting position and patted the bed next to himself. "Come, Lady, sit beside me," he said, his words a little slurred.

Doing as she was bid, Catherine wondered what new indignity was in store for her and was amazed when Charles put his arm around her shoulders and leant on her. He smiled and breathed wine fumes into her face. She forced herself not to draw back, a wife could be beaten for less, she knew.

"My Catherine," he said, "my little mouse." His free hand came up and stroked her hair. "You are so beautiful."

"You are drunk, Charles," she replied, her voice tinged with sadness.

"Oh yes," he answered. "Isn't it wonderful? The lady does not intimidate this drunken Charles."

"Intimidate? I?"

Charles planted a whiskery kiss on her cheek. "Indeed, Madam," he mumbled into her hair. "I, who, have killed many men in battle for my king, am intimidated by a little mouse of a girl." He began to sway backwards on the bed. "Ah, love can do such strange things to men and kings."

Catherine's breath caught in her throat. "Love, Sir?" she gasped.

Her question went unanswered. Charles had passed out. His body lay sprawled on the bed and his snores were loud enough to be heard throughout the castle.

Catherine gazed at him in wonder. Had he almost protested his love for her? For her; the little mouse? She brushed a lock of hair from his forehead, and he grasped her hand before she could remove it. Bringing it to his mouth he placed a gentle kiss on her palm, and then rolled onto his side and carried on snoring.

Tears that she had not known she could shed, spilled down her cheeks and sparkled in the candle-glow as she struggled to remove her husband's doublet and hose. He mumbled to himself as she moved him. She made out no words, but he had already said enough.

She knew that the dawn would bring forgetfulness, and it would be up to her to establish a new relationship with him. She may have been sold into this marriage by a greedy family, but she knew now that she was one of the lucky ones. Hers would be a marriage of love, for who could fail to love this big dolt, who needed to be in his cups in order to admit that he loved her.

Once she had made him comfortable, she climbed onto the bed and snuggled against his body. She lifted her head and kissed him tenderly. "Charles," she whispered, "I love you, too."

THE AUTHOR SAYS...

"Tudor times have always fascinated me. At school I once gave a presentation on Henry's six wives. Was it inevitable that some day I would write this story?"

Carrot Cake Squares

This recipe is gluten free, using polenta and ground almonds.

Ingredients (Makes 16 squares)

+ **125g butter, at room temperature**
+ **125g light muscovado sugar**
+ **4 eggs, beaten**
+ **Finely grated zest of 1 orange**
+ **150g ground almonds**
+ **150g instant polenta**
+ **1½tsp gluten-free baking powder**
+ **200g carrots, finely grated**

To decorate:

+ **300g low-fat soft cheese**
+ **2tbsp icing sugar**
+ **1tsp lemon juice**
+ **Small icing carrots (optional)**

1 Preheat the oven to 190°C, Fan Oven 170°C, Gas Mark 5. Grease and line a 23cm square cake tin.

2 Cream the butter and sugar together until light, then gradually beat in the eggs. Stir in the orange zest.

3 Mix together the ground almonds, polenta and baking powder. Stir into the creamed mixture with the carrots. Transfer to the cake tin and spread out evenly.

4 Bake in the centre of the oven for 35min, or until firm to the touch. Cool in the tin.

5 Cut the cake into 16 squares. Mix the low-fat soft cheese, icing sugar and lemon juice together, then spread on top of each square, topping each one with an icing carrot, if using.

Cook's Tip: You get a nicer finish if you decorate each square separately.

PHOTOGRAPHY: JONATHAN SHORT RECIPES AND FOOD STYLING: SUE ASHWORTH

Away From It All

Can Josh and Emma find a way to help their parents
put some much-needed zing back into their marriage?

By Linda Sainty

I t was Emma's idea to meet up with Josh for a quiet drink in town. She hadn't seen much of her brother in the past few months what with a new husband, new house and new job to keep her busy. Inevitably, given the time of year, the subject of their Mum's birthday had come up.

"I haven't got a clue," Josh remarked.

"I know," agreed Emma. "The trouble is, she's got everything."

"And what she hasn't got she doesn't want," put in Josh.

The two of them sipped their wine in unison and sighed. Their mother had to be the most difficult person in the world to

then. Or another cookbook. Boring."

"Well, if it makes Mum, happy…"

Emma took another sip of wine.

"Actually," said Josh, straightening, "I don't think Mum's looked happy for ages. I don't think either of them have, to be honest – not when they're together."

"Really?" Emma was genuinely taken aback. She had never thought of her parents in terms of happy or unhappy, she had just thought of them as… well, Mum and Dad. "What makes you say that?"

"Little things I've picked up when I've visited," Josh replied.

"Such as?" Emma felt uncomfortable. Since she'd moved away from her home town after her marriage to Ben a year ago she hadn't visited her parents nearly as

Their father didn't even feign delight when they presented him with an expensive gift

buy for. Apart from their father, of course. Their father didn't even feign delight when they presented him with a new sweater, shirt or bottle of expensive aftershave at Christmas or on his birthday.

"What about some designer lingerie," suggested Josh half-heartedly.

"Mum? Lingerie?" Emma looked at him. "That's a bit personal, Josh." Anyway, they were talking about Mrs Sensible, here – the woman who bought her underwear from the same well-known department store for years, always on the basis of durability and comfort, rather than style.

"Dad might like it though," said Josh.

"It's not Dad's birthday – it's Mum's," Emma reminded him, blushing.

"Hmm," Josh pouted. "It'll just have to be a voucher for the garden centre again,

often as she used to. Had she missed something important?

"They put on a good show, but I get the feeling it *is* just a show. There's a coldness in the house, a distance between them…" he tailed off. "Sometimes I wonder if the only thing they had in common was us, and now we've left…"

"Oh, Josh!" Emma put her hands over her ears, a little mannerism she'd had since a child when she didn't want to hear anything unpleasant. "Please don't tell me they're splitting up!"

"It happens, Em. Children fly the nest and the parents suddenly find there's nothing to keep them together and they start to drift apart."

Emma thought of her father – who'd

Continued overleaf

Continued from previous page

recently taken up running. It had been a source of amusement that the running sessions usually ended up at the local pub. Suppose it was just a cover for an affair? What if he was having a passionate fling with a barmaid from the pub? He was still an attractive man – and fit for his age.

Now she thought of it, wasn't there a little twinkle in his eye the last time she saw him, or had she imagined it? Hadn't her mother made a joke about his sudden conversion to male grooming products?

"I can't believe it," Emma said, pouring himself another glass of wine "Do you think Dad's cheating on Mum?"

"Dunno. He might be – but I doubt it."

house but there's been a definite glow about Mum of late."

Were they talking about the same woman? Mrs Duffel Coat and Comfy Walking Shoes? The only glow Emma could recall was a rosy tinge in her cheeks when she'd taken Freddie for a walk.

"Mum's not like that," she said.

"So what's Mum like – underneath that quiet exterior? Remember how she used to read us poetry when we were little? Dad didn't get it. Just as Mum didn't get Dad's obsession with doing up old cars. Maybe their differences opened up a big gap between them and…"

"And what?"

"Mum met someone new, a soul mate."

Her mother made a joke about his sudden conversion to male grooming products

"Well, I gather from Mum he's a bit of as regular at the Three Horseshoes these days. It's the perfect opportunity to meet someone. Dad might be getting on but he's still got it."

"So has Mum – in a more understated way," said Josh defensively.

Emma laughed. "But I can't imagine Mum… well, can you?"

"You know what they say about the quiet ones," said Josh staring into his glass. "There might be a coldness in the

"Are you saying that you think *Mum's* having an affair?"

"I didn't say that but it's possible."

"Wow!" Emma flung the menu down. "But how… when… with whom?"

"Maybe she's met someone on her walks with Freddie."

"Someone into Blake and Byron? That would be a bit of a tall order."

"But not impossible."

"No, nothing's impossible," Emma said, with a sigh as she stared disconsolately into her empty glass. She looked at the menu and then flung it down. "I'm not hungry anymore, Josh."

"Me neither."

"We need to sort this out," said Emma. "We can't let them drift apart. There's too much history between them and – bottom line – they love each other."

"Are you sure they do?" Josh mused.

"I'm not sure of anything at the moment. Apart from that I don't think we should be buying Mum a new cookbook for her birthday."

"You're right – so what then?"

Emma thought for a moment. "I've got an idea."

"A whole one?"

She flung the menu at him. "Listen to me, Josh – because I think this idea might just work for Mum's birthday – and I'm not talking Wincyette nighties or a year's subscription to a gardening magazine."

"Right," said Ben. "Shoot."

They were at the airport waiting for the plane from Venice. Two joyous, suntanned people ran towards them.

"How did it go?" asked Emma.

"Fabulous!"gushed her mother. "Your dad enjoyed looking at the architecture and discussing the vagaries of the Venetian drainage system and I retraced the steps of Byron and went on a tour of Shakespeare's Venice – it really was absolutely magical!"

"Great," said Josh. "So did you two, er… actually spend any time together?"

Their parents exchanged a strange look and smiled.

"Every evening, drinking wine on the veranda of our hotel as we gazed over the Grand Canal."

"Or taking a gondola to a restaurant in the evening."

"Or wandering through the old streets holding hands as the sun set – very romantic," confided their mother.

"Like a second honeymoon," their father announced, squeezing her hand.

"Yes," put in their mother with a grin. "But definitely not second best…"

"Too much information!" Emma said, grabbing her mother's case as they made their way out of the airport.

After they took their parents home, Josh dropped Emma at the train station.

"They seem to have had a great time," Emma remarked. "The holiday seems to have rekindled something between them." She looked at her brother. "Do you think they were having affairs?"

"No. I asked Dad straight out when you were upstairs helping Mum to unpack. The simple truth is, one day when Mum was out walking Freddie, she met a woman who belonged to a book club and Mum asked to join. Dad went to the Three Horseshoes for a bit of company because, from then on, Mum always had her head in a book and he got a bit lonely."

"So there was nothing really going on – no extra-marital romances?"

"Apparently not – but they were definitely drifting apart."

"In which case, the holiday in Venice was a bit of a master stroke on my part," Emma said, allowing herself a smug smile.

"Absolutely," agreed Josh. "Although I think you should give me some credit in putting back the zing in their relationship."

"In what way?"

"Well, when Mum was packing I slipped an extra present into her suitcase when she wasn't looking. It cost a small fortune, but designer lingerie doesn't come cheap, you know…"

THE AUTHOR SAYS…

"Children growing up and leaving home can be a difficult time for parents and the 'empty nest syndrome' can put a strain on relationships – not just for parents, but grown up children as well!"

Sweets For My Sweet

An unexpected meeting was set to rekindle school memories – but they were all older and wiser, now…

By Christine Evans

I became disillusioned with men when I was nine years old. Life was very bewildering as a naive only child.

My best friend Mandy had two older sisters and was worldly wise. It was Mandy who suggested we buy the love heart sweets with my pocket money. She didn't have any money for sweets and Mum gave me some to buy sweets on the way home from school.

Mandy's sisters were supposed to collect her but as she lived near to us she came home with me and Mum.

"Are you opening them love hearts, Alison? Here, let me see," Mandy said, grabbing them.

She started reading a sweet.

"You are a door…" she said puzzled.

"That's silly," I said giggling. "I'm not a door. Let me see."

I took the now grubby sweet from her sticky hand.

"You are adorable!" I read in triumph.

Mum and Dad often read to me and I was a good reader for my age.

"I am adorable," I said grinning at Mandy.

She shook her head, eager to enlighten me.

"It's not you what's adorable, Alison," she said. "It's your boyfriend. You give him this love heart to say he's adorable."

"I haven't got a boyfriend," I said.

"Well give it to the boy you like best and then he's your boyfriend," she said, exasperated by my ignorance.

"Right," I said, still bewildered.

I was sorry I hadn't bought jelly babies and just eaten them.

I took the next sweet out and read it. "Smitten" it said. We didn't know what smitten meant.

"Perhaps it's like a kitten," I suggested.

We read more bewildering messages and had almost finished the packet when Mum called me indoors. I popped the last few into my schoolbag.

I remembered what Mandy had said and knew which boy I liked best. Derek Digby was the biggest rogue in our class. Being a joker he made everyone laugh. Even Miss Cartright smothered a giggle

Continued overleaf

sometimes at his antics. Derek was good at football too. He spent more time thinking about that than his lessons. He wasn't the brightest button in the box, or so we thought when Miss Cartright taught us our times tables and then tested us.

"I can't remember things Miss," said Derek glumly, unable to answer yet another question.

"What were the names of the footballers who played in the recent semi-final," asked our teacher casually.

Derek reeled off all the names in an instant.

"You're not a stupid boy Derek, just a lazy one," she decided. "Buck up your ideas."

He scowled at her and scurried off after Derek. I blushed furiously, my humiliation complete.

I didn't bother with boys for ages, conscious of that first rejection, though my teens were full of crushes on pop stars. They were unobtainable and didn't pose a threat to my battered ego. So rather that spend time pining over boys I did well in my exams and went on to study nursing like my mum.

I didn't see Derek for ages, except when his picture appeared in the local paper as a star of our town's football team.

Then early one morning I reported for duty at our local hospital and a familiar

"I don't want to be your soppy boyfriend," he shouted, throwing down the sweet

He looked downhearted. We loved our pretty teacher and being told off in front of the class was humiliating. I decided to cheer him up with a love heart.

"Here you are Derek," I said handing him a sweet.

"Sweet…" he tried to read the message in its sugary heart.

"It says 'sweety pie'," I said proudly. "Now you can be my boyfriend."

He stared at me horrified.

"I don't want to be your soppy boyfriend," he shouted, throwing down the sweet in disgust, stalking away with his hands in his pockets.

His sidekick Gary bent to pick up the sweet.

"Eeugh! It's been on the ground," said Mandy, who'd witnessed all this.

name was listed on the new arrivals.

"Derek Digby," I read aloud.

"Yeah, he's something of a local football hero," said my colleague. "He has a compound fracture of his right leg."

"He was in my class at primary school," I told her.

She looked impressed.

Derek was in the ward looking miserable, his leg encased in plaster. I'd never realised how good looking he was before. His newspaper pictures didn't do him justice though I knew he was a local heartthrob.

"Hello Derek," I said smiling. "I bet you don't recognise me."

As he hadn't seen me in ages it was a daft thing to say. He looked me over.

"You're not that girl that threw her

LOVE HEART

"Shouldn't you be in a private hospital?" I asked him.

He grinned.

"That's Premier League players," he said chuckling. "I couldn't afford it on my salary. But I hope to join a major team." He gave me an appraising glance and smiled. "Anyway, I bet the nurses in the private hospitals aren't as pretty as the ones in this ward."

"Derek Digby, you old flatterer!" I said laughing. "No wonder all these girls try to smuggle themselves in to see you."

"I don't know why," he said puzzled. "They don't know me or anything. You and me go back a long way."

"To when you told me you didn't want to be my soppy boyfriend and chucked my love heart in the mud," I reminded him.

"Did I?" he asked, looking surprised. Mooning about Miss Cartright, he'd completely forgotten about it.

"I wouldn't now though," he said smiling. "Buy me all the love hearts you like and I'd savour every one."

"In your dreams!" I teased him.

To be honest I didn't really mean that but for ages I'd wanted to take revenge for his very first rejection. Whoever said "revenge is sweet" was quite wrong. I'd just missed a good opportunity to get to know him better.

"Do they make love hearts any more?" I asked.

"Oh yes," he said eagerly. "My brother had special ones for his wedding."

program at me and poked me in the eye," he said grumpily. "That's how I tripped in the tunnel and broke my leg. Luckily it was after the match."

"That wasn't me," I said. "I'm Alison Davison. I was in Miss Cartright's class with you."

He stared at me.

"No wonder I didn't recognise you. It's been some time. She was gorgeous though, Miss Cartright. My favourite teacher – my first love."

His face changed with dreamy remembrance. No wonder my measly love heart had been rejected. He loved our teacher!

My colleague was right about him being a local heartthrob, though. From the moment the report of his injury hit the local newspaper the cards and flowers began arriving.

Then star struck girls claiming to be his sisters or his cousins tried to get into the ward to see him. Local reporters wanted to interview him. He was moved into a side ward.

Another vaguely familiar face visited Derek the next day. Gary, his old sidekick, was tucking into a big bunch of grapes.

Continued overleaf

"Here's the gorgeous nurse, Alison Davison. We've been talking about you," he said.

"Obviously," I said laughing.

We reminisced about old teachers and classmates until the sister arrived asking for assistance.

"I wish you'd pay as much attention to the other patients as you do to Derek Digby nurse," she said. "I didn't take you for a silly fan. Anyway he might not receive so much attention in the future. The specialist mentioned this morning that Derek may never play professional football again."

I felt so sorry for him. Football was his whole life and he'd been tipped to join a major team. How could I face him knowing what I did? I listened hopefully for any sign that his career might be saved. But after a consultation with the specialist I found Derek looking miserable.

"I expect you've heard," he said, his eyes suspiciously red.

I wanted to fold him in my arms and comfort him but instead I held his hand and squeezed it.

"It isn't the end of the world," I said softly. "You've so much more to give."

"Like what," he said angrily. "I'm just a dumb footballer. Football is my life – was my life."

"I know. I remember how you reeled off all those footballers' names in class, but couldn't remember your times tables." I looked at him thoughtfully. "You know, with your memory for statistics you'd be a great football commentator."

He looked surprised.

"A local radio station asked me to provide a commentary for a league match

once when I had a hamstring injury and couldn't play."

"Did you do it?" I asked.

He shook his head.

"I didn't think I was clever enough."

"Of course you are Derek," I encouraged him. "Why don't you get in touch with the producer again. They'd give you training. Who knows where it might lead. You've got the face for television too."

He gave me a thoughtful look.

"Do you think so?"

"Are you fishing for compliments?" I asked chuckling. "Don't expect any. I'm still crushed about that rejected love heart."

"I thought about no-one else but Miss Cartright," he said. "I wanted to marry her when I grew up."

The sister summoned me.

"You're giving our Mr Digby undue attention again nurse," she reprimanded me, then her face softened. "In the circumstances it's quite permissible. He's certainly brighter than he was after the specialist's visit."

That gave me an idea. One of our old teachers was headmistress at our old school. Mandy's sisters had children at the school and mentioned it when we'd stopped for a chat. So I contacted her and she said she was still in touch with Miss Cartright.

"She's Jean Lawrence now," she told me. "Derek Digby, you say? What a rogue idea. My husband has some contacts in local radio. He'll put in a word for Derek."

I thanked her from the bottom of my heart. Derek was chuffed too.

"She wanted some autographs for her two kids. Miss Cartright asked me!"

He progressed well after that morale booster. I was sorry to see him go home though. He'd been a popular patient, always laughing and joking. Everyone gathered round to see him off so I missed my chance to see him alone. The ward seemed very dull without him.

I thought that was the end of it, a brief flirtation with a boy who'd once rejected me, a case of history repeating itself. Then one afternoon a familiar figure stood by the nurses' station.

"Here she is!" said Derek grinning.

"It isn't the end of the world," I said softly. "You have so much more to give, Derek"

he was! He needs help? I'm sure Jean would be delighted."

Although nearly twenty years older our old teacher hadn't changed much and was still very attractive. She remembered me well.

"I knew you'd do well Alison," she said.

I took her to see Derek.

"I've a visitor for you Derek," I said with a grin.

His face lit up when he saw our old teacher. She stayed with him for ages and from the laughter echoing from the ward, her pep talk was going well.

"I hope I've done some good," she told me as she was leaving. "Yours was a good

He was on his crutches, holding something in his hand.

"I have some problems getting about," he said, "but I've bought you something."

He placed a packet of love hearts in my hand.

"I'm sorry for what I did all those years ago. I haven't opened them but there'll be some sweets in there asking you to be my girl. If that's what you want?" he added humbly.

"Derek Digby I certainly do," I said. "If I wasn't on duty I'd kiss you."

"What time do you finish?" he asked with a grin.

I couldn't wait to end that shift and become the sweetheart of a sweet man.

Young Hearts Run Free...

Karen and Carly have their whole life planned out – until chance leads them down a different path

By Susan Sarapuk

K aren and I lay side by side in the summer grass as the radio played Candi Staton and we belted out the words that had become our anthem. I didn't really understand about counting up the years filled with tears but we knew that we were going to run free, that our lives were going to be exciting.

You'll get your baby but you won't get your man! we sang.

"I wouldn't mind having David's baby one day," Karen said. "If he met me we'd fall in love."

"Not if he met me first," I quickly said. We'd both been in love with David Cassidy for the past couple of years. "Anyway, I thought we weren't going to get married."

"True. I don't want to be tied down," Karen agreed. "I wouldn't want to marry any of the boys in our year. Yuk!"

"Yuk!" I agreed, but I think she fancied someone. I'd seen her looking at Alex Brown across the classroom.

As the song faded we contemplated in silence together.

The radio crackled in the background and bees buzzed among the clover. I rolled over on to my stomach and worked on splitting the stem of a tiny buttercup.

"Hey, look at those two!" a cry rang out, shattering our idyll.

I looked up to see Peter, Alex and Jonathan coming towards us.

"What are they doing? Maybe they're kissing!" Jonathan sneered.

"Get lost!" Karen said. "We're listening to the radio."

"Can we join you?" Peter sat down. Peter was OK; he was in most of my classes and sometimes he'd help me if I was struggling with something in maths.

Alex sat next to Karen while Jonathan hovered awkwardly.

"Who's your favourite band?" Peter asked us.

"We both like David Cassidy," Karen said. "We think he's gorgeous."

The three boys looked disdainful.

"Well, what's yours then?" Karen challenged them.

"The Who," Jonathan declared and the other two nodded.

That was the thing with boys – no taste at all, just an instinct for mindless noise.

"What are you doing here?" I said. "We were happy until you lot turned up."

Continued overleaf

Continued from previous page

"We've been playing football with some of the lads from Year 6," Peter explained. "Mr Moore from PE asked us to help out. We decided to take a shortcut home. We didn't know you were here."

He looked embarrassed, the way you do when you lie.

"Can't you turn this up any louder?" Jonathan said, fiddling with the radio.

"Go away and leave us alone!" Karen snatched it out of his hands.

"Yeah, go away," Alex suddenly turned on his friend.

"It's boring here, anyway," Jonathan shrugged and sloped off.

Peter lay back on the grass, hands

certainly making up for it now!

"I, er…" Peter stumbled over words and I turned back to him. "I didn't want to ask you in school because…" he looked embarrassed now. "Well, do you want to go out with me?"

For a moment I stared at him, shocked.

"We didn't know you were here." He looked embarrassed, the way you do when you lie

clasped behind his head. "I'm going up there one day," he said as he looked up at the sky.

"Where to?" I asked.

"Everywhere. I'm going to be a pilot. What about you?" He looked at me.

I'd never felt Peter Davies' attention on me before the way it was now. "I don't know, but we can be anything and go anywhere. We were just talking about that, weren't we?" I turned to Karen only to find her and Alex snogging each other. "Karen!" After all we'd said!

"Ignore them," Peter grinned. "Alex has had a thing for Karen for ages."

Five minutes ago we'd been singing about running free and vowing that no man was ever going to tie us down.

Maybe it's because neither of us had ever had a boyfriend, but Karen was

Then I could feel myself blushing.

"The fair's in town on the weekend," he said. "We could go there, if you like."

"OK," I agreed.

"Great! Meet you at Joe's café at six on Saturday. Come on Alex, time to go."

The radio was still playing in the background as we watched them leave. Then we looked at each other, both of us flushed with pleasure and surprise.

"What about young hearts running free and all that?" I protested.

"It's just a song," Karen said.

And I suppose it was.

THE AUTHOR SAYS…

"I was listening to this Candi Staton song on a CD and the image of the two young girls lying in the grass came to me."

Brain BOOSTERS

Sudoku

Fill in each of the blank squares with the numbers 1 to 9, so that each row, each column and each 3x3 cell contains all the numbers from 1 to 9.

1

				3	2	1		
		8						7
7		1		2				4
	9			7	3			8
2			6					
1		7					9	
8	1		2		7			
		5			1			
		9	6	3		8		

2

		1			2			
8					2			
		7				9	5	6
2		6					7	9
	9				5			3
7		8				2	1	
		2				3	6	5
	6				4			
	2			3				

Word Wheel

You have ten minutes to find as many words as possible using the letters in the wheel. Each word must be three letters or more and contain the central letter. Use each letter once and no plurals, foreign words or proper nouns are allowed. There is at least one nine-letter word.

Average: 42 words
Good: 43-63 words
Excellent: 64-84 words

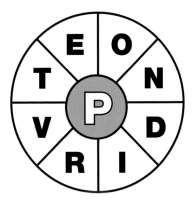

Passport To Happiness?

Louise knew what she wanted and had her life all mapped out – until a wild wind blew her off course…

By Claire Buckle

BOARDING PASS DENIED.' Louise frowned at the message on the laptop screen and entered Tim's passport number for a second time.

"What the…?" she grumbled. She'd had no problem checking herself in, but once again, there was the same dreaded response to her husband's details.

She got up from the kitchen table, rummaged in her handbag for her mobile phone and rang the airline's customer services. If it could be sorted out quickly, she'd still get to work on time.

"Your call is important to us. Please hold." The automated voice set her teeth on edge. She sat down, took a few deep, calming, yoga breaths, closed her eyes and let her thoughts wander.

It had taken bucket-loads of time and effort for Louise to organise their trip to Cape Cod. She'd compared sites for the best deals on flights, obsessed over reviews on accommodation and devised what she hoped would be a thrilling itinerary. Kayaking, horse riding and whale watching were all booked, and she'd allocated plenty of time for shopping.

Boy, did they need this holiday! Her job in Human Resources was hectic. She often worked late and was looking forward to a break from routine, but it was Tim who was most in need of a rest. Under his soft grey eyes, puffy dark circles had recently appeared and he'd started biting his nails again – a habit he'd kicked, along with smoking, after they left university more than ten years ago.

When he arrived home last night, he hadn't pulled her towards him for their usual hello kiss, nor had he mentioned the mouth-watering aroma of lamb shanks braising in the oven.

"Problems at work?" she asked, although she'd guessed the answer. He hadn't replied, but took a beer from the fridge, slumped into a kitchen chair and stared at the bottle as he rolled it back and forth in his palms.

"They're insisting I cut corners and breach health and safety to increase profits, but I just won't do it."

Lou had tried to push thoughts of the expensive holiday and dreams of moving to one side. Tim was a site manager at a

Continued overleaf

Continued from previous page
construction company and worked to the highest principles. She wouldn't have it otherwise but couldn't ignore the fact that he was earning more than they imagined possible at this stage of his career.

With the huge bonus he'd been promised on the completion of the apartments and their combined salaries, they'd be able to move out of the maisonette and into a house in sought-after Mill Road. Of course, they'd have to put off having children for a few more years, but still…

Tim's voice halted her racing thoughts. "I phoned Steve at the recruitment agency. He's fixed an interview for me,

"Of course. I'm just tired and hungry," he replied, but his eyes avoided hers.

A cheerful voice brought Lou back to the present. "Good morning, Melanie speaking, how can I help?"

"At last," Lou said, glancing at her watch and realising several minutes had passed. She explained the situation.

"Has your husband applied for a new passport since the last time you travelled to the States?"

Lou bit her lip. "We were in New York last year. It expired after we got back."

"He needs to reapply for a new visa through ESTA, the Electronic System for Travel Authorisation," Melanie said.

Louise silently berated herself. How could she have overlooked something so simple?

tomorrow at two o'clock."

Lou had folded her arms and leaned against the kitchen counter, letting out a shaky breath. "How will you get away from work?"

Tim had shrugged. "I'll say I've a doctor's appointment or dentist."

"What, out of the blue just before we go on holiday? Won't they be suspicious?" She opened the oven door and checked the lamb. Her appetite was diminishing as fast as the knot in her stomach was tightening.

"I don't want you to worry, Lou, this is my problem. Let's just look forward to the holiday. I'm just sorry I didn't get time to help you sort it out."

"It's fine, I enjoyed it." She shut the oven door and scanned his face. "Are you sure nothing else is wrong?"

Lou tried to keep her cool. "Tim and I had valid ESTAs for New York. I thought they lasted two years."

"They do, but a new passport needs a new ESTA."

Louise silently berated herself. How could she have overlooked something so simple?

"But how long will that take? Our flight leaves in the morning," Louise asked, trying to keep panic at bay.

"I can't say definitely, but the website states anything up to 72 hours."

Louise swallowed hard, trying to dislodge what felt like a stone in her throat. "I'd better get on with it, then," she said, hoarsely.

She found the website and paid the fee. Already running late, she'd just have to hope she could print the pass later.

How did the interview go?" Lou asked Tim. She was surprised to come home from work and find him changed and watching TV. "Didn't you go back to the site afterwards?"

"No, I didn't bother and actually, it went really well. The director seemed a nice guy."

She sat on the arm of the sofa. Tim muted the TV and turned to look at her. He hesitated before he said,

"There's just one thing about the job… they don't pay as much, but what's most important is they're a more ethical company and seem to care about their employees."

"Fine." She hadn't meant to sound so abrupt, but the most pressing problem of the boarding pass had been playing on her mind all day.

"It probably happens a lot," Tim said, after she explained. "Come on, we'll try printing it now, then order a takeaway and finish packing. I can't wait to get away."

Louise had felt the tenseness in her shoulders ease, as the printer had clunked awake and the pass printed. It was a sign of a corner being turned she decided, although by the time they'd endured a four-hour delay at the airport, a long queue through security and for car hire at Boston, plus a GPS which directed them up a wooded lane and onto private land, she was having second thoughts.

Luckily, the free map in the glove compartment put them on the right road, the keys were in a box outside the realtor's office and by late afternoon Tim drove through open wooden gates to their rented cottage.

Louise peered through the windscreen and couldn't keep the disappointment from her voice. "It's not quite what I was expecting…"

In her head she was already composing a complaint to post on the website.

Tim rubbed the back of his neck and let out a deep sigh. "It's fine, Lou. We haven't even seen inside yet."

It had looked lovely online. In reality, the cream weatherboarding needed a good scrub down, the driveway needed weeding and the deck could have done with a varnish.

Tim unloaded the cases and stood behind Lou as she opened the door.

She let out a surprised gasp. "Oh, Tim – it's gorgeous!"

In the open-plan living space, the afternoon sun sliced through half-open shutters at long windows, tinting a whitewashed table and chairs a magical gold. Cushions patterned with seabirds and anchors were scattered on a pebble coloured sofa and bright paintings of sailboats and lobster pots hung on pale apricot walls.

Tim mumbled in agreement and went through to the bedroom. Lou followed. The bed was covered with a multi-coloured patchwork quilt, on which he placed the cases and began unpacking.

Continued overleaf

Continued from previous page

"Are you alright? You seem…" she tried to pinpoint his mood, "distracted."

Usually, as soon as they arrived at their destination, he liked to kick off his shoes, relax and leave the unpacking until later.

"I'm fine. Why wouldn't I be? I'm married to a beautiful woman and we're about have a fabulous holiday. What more could I want?"

He smiled but it looked forced and she couldn't stop the words tumbling out.

"For the company to listen to you. Make them pay attention. You deserve that position." She almost added, *and the salary, too.*

The smile vanished and in its place a muscle pulsed in his jaw. Let's leave it, can we? Let's just have a good time."

Easier said than done Lou thought, unzipping her case, but she'd have to try.

earning. What about sticking it out where you are, at least until you've looked round a bit more?"

He shook his head. "No, Lou. This company are building eco-friendly houses, something I'm much more interested in than million pound flats. I thought you'd be pleased. It's still a decent wage, but it seems all you're bothered about these days is the money."

She saw bewilderment in his face and felt a twist of hurt in the pit of her stomach. How could he think it was money she mostly cared about? Then again, why wouldn't he? She'd been the one who pushed for expensive, jam-packed holidays and an executive-style house. She'd even been willing to put off having a family for a better postcode.

Tears stung her eyes. "That's not true. I love you and I'm with you all the way,

She saw the bewilderment in his face and felt a twist of hurt in the pit of her stomach

Louise stirred in bed and squinted at the clock. 6a.m. To her surprise, when she rolled over, Tim's side was empty. She put on her silky dressing gown and padded barefoot into the living area. Tim was in his pyjama bottoms, sitting on the sofa, staring at his phone.

"What are you doing?" she said through a yawn as she sat beside him.

"I've just had an e-mail from Steve. I've been offered the job, Lou," he replied with a grin.

"Great," she said, wide-awake at the news. However, when he told her the salary, she groaned.

"But Tim, that's way below what you're

Tim. Please believe me."

He blew out his cheeks. "That's a relief because they want me to start two days after we get back."

"But won't you need to give a month's notice?" she asked, baffled.

He put his phone on the coffee table and looked sheepish when he said, "Not any more. The day before the interview, I walked out."

"What?" She managed to splutter. "Why didn't you tell me?"

"Because I didn't want to worry you, or spoil the holiday. I had a big row with the director, cleared my desk and left. I was so angry. I walked around the streets for

ages. I needed to sort it in my head."

Lou shook her head, trying to absorb the news.

"And what if you hadn't got the job? Would you have pretended to go to work every day?" A while back she'd watched a TV drama about a man who'd been made redundant and did just that.

He shrugged. "Maybe," he said.

"Oh, Tim. I don't want you to protect me from the truth, even if you think it's for the right reasons. Promise me you'll never do something like that again."

He hesitated before he tenderly replied, "OK, I'm sorry. I know we've always promised there'd be no secrets."

A warm glow of relief spread through her. She threaded her arm through his and leaned on his warm bare shoulder. From a basket of shells on the coffee table, a delightful scent reminiscent of sea spray drifted upwards.

"Tim?"

"What?"

"What are those eco-houses like?"

"Very nice and surprisingly affordable. All solar panels, bamboo flooring and sustainable cladding," he said. "They're not Mill Road though," he added in a serious voice.

About to explain she didn't care about Mill Road, she lifted her head and saw his wry smile. It was then she noticed a driftwood sign, hanging high up on the wall behind him.

We cannot direct the winds, but we can adjust our sails, it said.

"They sound perfect," she murmured and as his lips touched hers, an image came into her mind of them decorating a nursery in their pretty cedar-clad house.

Whatever the future had in store, she knew her passport to happiness was right here beside her.

● ●

THE AUTHOR SAYS...

"The saying, 'one thing after another' sparked the idea, as did my experience of renting a cottage in Provincetown, Cape Cod, which had a tatty exterior, but inside was just perfect!"

To Suit An Angel

With her family grown, Rachel longed to feel needed
again which was why the job ad was perfect for her…

By Stella Whitelaw

The advertisement in the Situations Vacant column of the prestigious morning newspaper stood out. The stark white border threw into prominence the large, dark type of the first three words:

ANGEL REQUIRED
URGENT
Managing Director of small progressive firm requires Personal Assistant of unique calibre.
Essential qualifications: a sense of humour and the patience of an angel. Initiative, dependability, able to make own decisions and work under pressure.

Rachel read the advertisement twice, sipping her cooling coffee. She was no angel, never had been. It conjured up the vision of an immaculately dressed woman in a pristine white suit, cream shoes, pale silk shirt with long fair hair, of course. She would create order out of chaos. Her smile would be sweet, her voice melodious. She would be an admirable woman, perfect in every way.

Rachel was so different. She stretched in her armchair. Ten-thirty already and she had finished her day's chores. She'd answered all the emails, placed the grocery orders, returned any phone calls, put a chicken casserole in a slow cooker.

An empty morning stretched ahead of her and an empty afternoon. The advertisement sounded so different, so friendly. How wonderful to be needed so much. It was a long time since she had felt needed.

Her home almost ran itself. The children were grown up and had left the nest. Harry was always away, days at a time, often abroad. When he was at home, he shut himself in his study, tired out, spent hours on the phone. He had forgotten she existed, barely spoke to her.

The more money Harry made, the less time they spent together. Once it hadn't been like this. Once they had shared a life and weekends had been fun and the arrival of both children a mutual joy.

Rachel felt a surge of excitement. It would be so simple to arrange. She would be back in the evening long before he came home, table laid, cooking supper.

She sat in front of her computer. The advertisement said apply by email.

Dear Sir,
I have been an angel for quite a few years, running a home, bringing up children, organising a household under pressure, making all the decisions. I have

Continued overleaf

Continued from previous page

red hair but no-one says that angels have to be blonde. I have my own car, so no wings required, only a parking space.

She signed it with her maiden name. She already felt different, younger, full of energy, more capable in every respect.

Rachel did not expect a reply so soon. A return email came the next morning asking her to attend an interview in two days time.

She sent an affirmative reply. No wasted words. Angels didn't waste words.

She didn't look like an angel. Her suit was a navy pin-stripe, her shirt crimson silk, her shoes flat navy slip-ons. Her hair was twisted up into a top-knot and pinned with clips. The only angelic touch were the pearl earrings which Harry had given her on their tenth anniversary.

The office building in the city was a tower of glass, perfect for angels to fly in and out of if they had a head for heights. The lift took her silently up to the sixteenth floor.

Rachel was escorted to the managing director's office, along a well-lit corridor. His office was at the furthermost end, almost falling off the building. He was sitting behind a mahogany desk, writing with a thin gold-nib pen. Rachel saw that his dark hair was heavily flecked with grey. He looked up, startled. His tired eyes blinked at her.

"I'm applying for the job of angel."

"Sorry, you surprised me for a moment. I wasn't expecting a real angel."

"Well, trust me I know how an angel works. I could take care of your office, your trips abroad, your home life."

"Home life?"

"I'm guessing that you fall asleep exhausted. You don't even notice if your wife is around."

"So you're psychic too?"

"I'm an angel, remember?"

He began to laugh. "You talk a lot of sense. The job is yours if you want it."

"Yes, I want it," said Rachel. "I think I'm needed." A warmth was stealing through her.

"Can you start soon?" he asked.

"I can start tomorrow."

"Perfect," he said. "So we could have lunch today and talk about your duties and salary, of course."

"Thank you," said Rachel. "Lunch would be very pleasant. I'm glad to see that you are still using the gold-nib pen that I gave you."

"And you are wearing the pearl earrings that I gave you," said Harry. A smile came into his eyes and some of the years fell away. "I can't believe I didn't recognise our own email address."

"Another sign you need my help."

"Shall I tell my staff that my wife is an angel?"

"Oh, I think they'll know soon enough," Rachel grinned.

THE AUTHOR SAYS...

"I had always thought it would be fun to work for my husband, who was clever and funny, but without him knowing it was me. I would have to go in disguise, perhaps as an angel. Inspirations are always difficult to pin down. This was a day dream really."

BRAIN BOOSTER SOLUTIONS

CODEBREAKER from page 35

PHRASE: BRIDGET JONES'S DIARY

KRISS KROSS from page 63

MISSING LINK from page 97

ACROSS: 1 Pass 3 Physical 8 Train 9 Album 11 Lunch 12 Eternal 14 Star 16 Cups 20 Emperor 22 Melba 24 Proof 26 Tenor 27 Audience 28 Seat
DOWN: 1 Puzzle 2 Satin 4 Hunter 5 Share 6 Cob 7 Father 10 Milk 13 Nap 15 Tip 16 Coming 17 Deep 18 Arctic 19 Market 21 Rifle 23 Large 25 Old
SHADED WORD: ZIPPED

SUDOKU 1 from page 151

6	5	8	4	7	3	2	1	9
9	4	2	8	1	6	5	3	7
7	3	1	5	9	2	6	8	4
5	9	4	1	2	7	3	6	8
2	8	3	9	6	4	1	7	5
1	6	7	3	5	8	4	9	2
8	1	6	2	4	9	7	5	3
3	2	5	7	8	1	9	4	6
4	7	9	6	3	5	8	2	1

SUDOKU 2 from page 151

6	5	1	4	9	2	7	3	8
9	8	7	3	5	6	2	1	4
4	2	3	7	1	8	9	5	6
2	1	4	6	3	5	8	7	9
8	9	6	1	2	7	5	4	3
7	3	5	8	4	9	6	2	1
1	7	9	2	8	4	3	6	5
3	6	8	5	7	1	4	9	2
5	4	2	9	6	3	1	8	7

WORDWHEEL from page 151
The nine-letter word is PROVIDENT

Dancing Queen

The things one does in the course of the job – learning to dance, flirting madly, coming back down to earth…

By Lydia Jones

O K, Fay – country dancing for you." My editor, speaking in shorthand as usual, beams. "Town's seven hundredth anniversary – midsummer dances on West Common are being revived."

"Dancing? Me?"

"Paper will have two ongoing projects showing we're part of community celebrations. I want blogs on the website; videos… Jeremy is doing steam railway restoration, so you get dancing."

"Isn't that – a little sexist?" I smile so I don't seem stroppy. My colleague/competitor, Jeremy, smirks in a way that makes me want to smack him.

"No, Fay. Dancing is on your CV."

That'll be the CV on which I bigged up any hobby I'd ever had.

"And Jeremy will be stripping and greasing engines."

Fair enough. Point taken.

"I need someone for bigger stories. Whoever shines with this could get more."

So no pressure.

My editor retreats to his man-cave; Jeremy continues to smirk.

Dancing shoes on, then.

C ould be fun," my friend, Hannah says engouragingly. "Cute primary children! You're bound to get good copy."

Except that they're not cute. They're stroppy teenagers.

When I arrive, boys are running an archetypal grey-haired Morris-man ragged, giggling and clattering sticks.

"Lads!" An authoritative voice shouts. "That's enough!"

I watch astounded as they almost stand to attention. The Voice, attached to a Greek-God-in-a-tracksuit, strides forward.

"Carl Jackson." He shakes my hand as I try to recall my name or anything intelligent to say. "Head of PE. This crew are mine. They're not bad when you know them."

I'm loving the way his eyes widen when he talks. Is he flirting just a little?

"How did you persuade them?"

I twinkle back a little, just in case.

"It's a boys' school – I promised them there would be girls."

I follow his gaze to a group of pretty specimens, self-consciously hair-flicking.

"Very Machiavellian."

"I do my best."

Yep. Definitely flirting. Oh, goody.

"Come on, Sir – you need a partner too."

Continued overleaf

Continued from previous page

Carl puts out an arm to me. There are cat calls and whistling as I take it and my stomach flip-flops.

Dance Friday becomes my week's highlight as Carl and I master dances like *Blaydon Races, Strip The Willow* and ironically *The Love Knot.* When he swings me in his arms, I can't stop smiling.

Yet nothing happens. Is he just a flirt?

"You got her number yet, Sir?"

"Shut it, Zack, and get on the minibus." Carl smiles. "Sorry."

"S'OK."

I see a pretty redhead blush as Zack winks. I wish I could tell her the male

I'm afraid your muddy dance masterclass has gone viral," Hannah says.

I groan. "How do I face them?"

"Fay, you're a fabulous newshound. No way can you let smarmy Jeremy win."

"Aaw, thanks Hannah."

"Besides you've only a week to get together with Greek-God."

Everyone applauds as I approach the final rehearsal, chin held high.

"You're well brave, Miss," the redhead says admiringly.

"Oh, you know. Thick-skinned," I say.

The kids have learned the dances well; next week's performance will be brilliant. I'll be sad for it to end. For many reasons.

Carl catches up with me in the car park.

Feet race in and out of the dance circle. I feel as if I'm flying. And then, suddenly, I am

mind gets easier to fathom.

"So, Fay." The Ed looms over my desk. "Dance video for the blog? Jeremy uploaded a brilliant piece yesterday."

"Dancing isn't like greasing an engine – you can't film yourself doing it."

"I could film you," Jeremy chirps.

"There – sorted." Ed smirks.

I stick mental pins in Jeremy.

So – like before." I smile at the pupils. "Ignore the camera."

Conscious of Jeremy, I'm possessed by some demon wanting to demonstrate prowess. Feet race in and out of the dance circle. I feel as if I'm flying.

And then I am. Colliding with Zack and partner I'm suddenly face-down in the field. Mud-smeared, I sit up and find Jeremy's phone in my face. Perfect.

"Fay – err – could we meet up? Properly – without the audience? I've wanted to ask, but the kids –"

"What did you have in mind?"

All of me is smiling.

"Maybe we could try one of those mud therapy sessions at the leisure centre?"

I swat him.

"Saracen's Head at seven?"

"OK."

"Great." He grins. "I've never been out with a famous film star before."

• •

THE AUTHOR SAYS...

"My local school has revived community country dancing. It's frenetic – I wondered how you'd get together with anyone in that situation so I decided I'd create characters who did."

Each Week in

My Weekly

- **Super Celebrities**
- **Up-to-date Health News**
- **Fabulous Fiction**

PLUS
- Puzzles • Cookery
- Fashion • Beauty
- Real Life

You'll Love It! On Sale Every Tuesday

The Perfect Present

Despite all of Eileen's blessings, there was only one thing she really wanted for Christmas...

By Norman Kitching

"Oh, how lovely," exclaimed Eileen as she extracted a woollen scarf from the holly and robin covered wrapping paper. "Just what I wanted."

"You say that every time, Gran," said Jake, her nine-year-old grandson.

"Well, that's because I mean it. A nice warm scarf is just what I need in this cold weather. I'm so glad you bought it for me."

She smiled to herself. What she said was partly true. She was quite happy to have a scarf to keep her warm but she wasn't sure about one with big blue and white stripes. It was just like the one Jake wore when he went to football with his dad.

"We never know what to buy you for Christmas," was the annual complaint from all her family. "When we ask what you'd like you always say that you've got everything you need."

In spite of the lack of guidance they always managed to come up with a few surprises, such as the DVD player that her son, Harry, gave her last year. She wasn't impressed with it at first, until she discovered that she could watch her favourite old films on it whenever she wanted. On the other hand she still hadn't worked out why she would need the pasta making machine that her daughter, Michelle, gave her three years ago. She always laughed when she spotted it at the back of the cupboard in the kitchen. At least, thought Eileen, she'd made an effort and bought something more than bath cubes.

Which was more than she could say as she looked at the presents she'd opened so far. As well as Jake's scarf there was a pair of gloves, some deodorants, a couple of book tokens and a box of her favourite chocolates. Not that she minded. She preferred money to be spent on presents for her grandchildren and was more interested in making sure that everyone else had a good Christmas.

"Mum's bought dad an iPad for Christmas," announced Jake as he draped the stripy scarf round Eileen's neck. "He's been dropping hints for weeks."

"Oh dear," said Eileen with a grin. "He'll look just like a pirate if he has an eye patch."

"Not an eye patch, Gran. An iPad. It's like a computer only ever so tiny. About as big as that photo on the mantelpiece. You can do all sorts of things with them. Dad's

Continued overleaf

Continued from previous page

upstairs now, getting it set up."

Eileen had actually heard about iPads and they sounded rather complicated. She tried to keep up with modern trends and had her own computer.

She'd got the hang of sending emails. The family were trying to get her to use internet searches but to Eileen that seemed like a step too far.

Having opened the last of her presents – another book token, some writing paper and a glass paperweight – she sat back and looked round at her family. Three children, their partners and seven grandchildren made a happy roomful.

Christmas lunch was, as always, a happy, noisy affair with a lot of chatter and joking. It was a bit of a squash getting everyone around the table but nobody minded. It was such a joy to be all together.

"Maybe I'll hear from her next year," said Eileen as she raised her glass.

"You don't need to wait that long, Mum," said Harry, grinning from ear to ear. "We keep telling you what a wonderful thing the internet is. We used it to trace Auntie Marjorie. Here's a little surprise for you."

An envelope was passed round the table to Eileen. She stared at it in

"Here's a little surprise for you." Eileen stared at the envelope in amazement

They were the most important thing in Eileen's life and she enjoyed being with them all, especially at Christmas.

"Penny for your thoughts, Mum," said her youngest daughter, Janice, who came and sat beside her.

"I was thinking about your Auntie Marjorie. I sent her a card as I always do but I haven't heard from her in twenty years. I do appreciate all the things you buy for me but a card from Marjorie would be the perfect present."

Eileen's sister went to live in Canada over forty years ago. The last time they'd seen each other was at their mother's funeral. There was a silly argument over a small piece of jewellery and after Marjorie went back to Canada all contact was lost.

Eileen regretted the argument, especially when the brooch in question turned out to be paste. She wrote several letters to Marjorie but got no reply.

amazement. The postmark showed that it was from Toronto in Canada.

"Go on, Gran," Jake called across the table. "Open it."

Eileen opened the envelope with trembling fingers and took out the Christmas card. Through her tears she read the greeting inside.

With fond memories and lots of love from Marjorie and family.

"How wonderful," said Eileen. "Just what I wanted. And she's put her new address on the card.

"I can write to her with the writing paper Lucy gave me."

"Emily's got a present she forgot to give you earlier," said Janice.

Eileen's youngest grandchild toddled round the dining table and handed her a small parcel.

"Happy Christmas, Grandma," she lisped. Inside the parcel was something

that looked like a plastic egg with one eye in the middle.

Eileen gave everyone a puzzled look.

"What is it?"

"You'll find out one day," said Michelle. "Then you'll wonder how you ever managed without one."

For the rest of the meal the conversation was full of anecdotes about Marjorie and other members of the family. The grandchildren were fascinated to hear about this new aunt who they'd never met. When the meal was finished and the table cleared Eileen sat back in her chair and looked around at her family.

"I think that was the best Christmas ever," she declared. "Thank you all so much."

"It's not over yet," said Harry as he got up and left the room. "Do excuse me for a minute or two."

Five minutes later he was back.

"Look what my new toy can do," he said as he placed his iPad in front of Eileen. She gasped as she looked at the tiny screen.

"That's Marjorie. How did you get a photo of her on that thing?"

"It's not a photo," said a tinny voice from the iPad. "It really is me. Merry Christmas Eileen."

"With the right kit you can use the internet to talk to people anywhere in the world," explained Harry. "Talk as long as you like. It doesn't cost a penny."

The two sisters chatted away happily for fifteen minutes. Twenty years of silly arguments just disappeared.

Talk to you again soon," said Marjorie finally. "Merry Christmas from all of us to all of you."

Eileen said her goodbyes then watched the little screen go blank.

"I still don't believe you can speak to someone in Canada using a computer."

"You'd better start believing," said Harry. "That funny little thing Emily gave you is a camera. I'll attach it to your computer and set it up then show you how to use it."

"You mean I can see Marjorie any time I want?"

"Yes, and at Easter you can see her for real," said Harry as he handed her an envelope. "In this envelope are the tickets. You sail to New York on the Queen Victoria then travel by train to Toronto."

"I don't know what to say," said Eileen. "I'm going to Canada. I don't believe it."

"It's cold in Canada," said Jake. "You'll need that scarf I gave you."

"You're right, Jake. That really was the perfect present."

THE AUTHOR SAYS...

"I have got to the age where I find it hard to say what I want for Christmas. So I wondered what someone else's perfect present would be."

Closing For Christmas

When two young people don't know what's best for them, you sometimes have to resort to any means...

By Mhairi Grant

C arly stretched, blinked her tired eyes and looked away from the computer screen and on to the street below. Under the sodium lights of the street lamps, the frost sparkled as vapour trails of breath followed Christmas shoppers in and out of the stores.

At least, Carly thought, she didn't have that hassle. She had no-one to shop for. Carly always tried to look on the positive side of things, and the number one positive thing on her list was the public library. It was her refuge and where she studied part-time for a business administration degree.

There was only one other person left and the library would close soon, but Carly didn't want to leave. It was warm in the library, whereas her bedsit was draughty. She almost had to sit on the electric fire to get any heat.

Carly let out a sigh.

Andy looked up from his newspaper. He thought that his shaking out and rustling the newspaper was the cause for her sigh. He hadn't meant to distract her, but he had a way of getting people's back up. People always wanted to pick a fight

with him. It was his size and his broken nose. The area that he had been brought up in was nicknamed Beirut and Andy had spent the better part of his adult life trying to put his past and his family's criminality behind him.

He didn't think that any member of his family had ever stepped over the threshold of a library and he wasn't about to tell them about his visits. He hardly saw them anyway. He worked in a gym and spent a lot of his spare time in the library, but it was about to close for the Christmas holidays.

A ndy looked at Angela behind her desk. He had a present for her. It was a thank you for all her help, but he didn't know how to give it to her. He wasn't used to giving presents.

Earlier the girl on the computer had given her a present. She had been so casual and dismissive about it and hadn't hung around for Angela's gratitude. It was almost as if she was embarrassed.

Andy realised that he should have given Angela the chocolates as soon as he'd come in, but now, it would seem as if it was a big thing and he didn't want his gift to be misconstrued.

After all, Angela was a married woman.

Just read this article, he thought, give Angela the damned chocolates and then go to the pub. He didn't really want to go to the pub, but he had nowhere else to go.

Andy let out a sigh.

Angela looked at Andy and then Carly. They were both regulars and as far as she was aware had never spoken to each other. It was a shame really. She had a soft spot for them both – and she had a sneaky feeling that they would get on like a house on fire.

Angela looked at the clock… twenty minutes to go. What on earth could she do

Continued overleaf

about them in twenty minutes?

Angela let out a sigh.

It drew Carly's attention. She wondered what caused it. Earlier, Angela had been excited about Christmas and had chatted about her husband and two boys and the preparations that she still had to do. It made Carly wonder what it would be like to have a family.

Carly had been brought up in care and had left the social system at sixteen and gone into a hostel, then got a job in Benny's Bingo.

She soon realised that if she was to make something of herself she would have to further her education, but she had flunked school and was frightened.

It had been Angela who had told her of the online courses available and had encouraged her all the way. Giving her the angel that lit up had been her way of

Angela will want to get home, so he had better go.

Carly closed down the computer. Angela had a life so she better make herself scarce. She reached for her coat.

Andy picked up his scarf.

They both froze when they heard a gasp. Angela had stumbled right into the Christmas tree.

"Angela!" They both ran to help.

"It's alright," she mumbled, "I just had a dizzy turn, that's all."

"Sit here," said Andy supporting her, "and put you head between your knees."

"I'll get you a glass of water," said Carly, going to the water cooler.

"I feel so silly," said Angela, accepting the water.

"Not at all," said Andy, hunkering down beside her. "You've probably been doing too much."

Carly was surprised at the concern in

Angela looked at the clock... there was only twenty minutes to go before closing

telling her how much she meant to her, but now Carly thought it just looked tacky.

Just one present, that's all she needed to buy – and she couldn't even get that right, could she?

Why, Andy thought, couldn't he have been more original? Quite a few of the punters had given Angela chocolates. He wasn't used to buying presents but she had been so good to him, keeping books by for him that she knew he would like, discussing literature with him and always making him feel welcome.

She deserved better.

Andy closed the paper in frustration.

his voice. She had always thought of him as a bit of a tough nut, but now that she looked at him she saw that he had the most kind and expressive eyes.

She took Angela's hand. "How are you getting home?"

"My husband will be here shortly, so I'll be fine."

"Is there anything we can do?" asked Andy, looking at Carly.

She really had the most beautiful blue eyes. He had never noticed them before as he mainly saw her from behind.

"Well… if you could just put a few books away and tidy up for me please, I

would be most grateful," Angela said.

"No problem," they both chorused, bumping into each other as they tried to grab the same books.

"I'll do the fiction and you do the non fiction," said Carly, looking up at Andy. He really was a big man, thought Carly, and all of it was muscle.

"Don't carry too much at once," replied Andy. The girl was just a titch of a thing and it made him feel protective.

Ten minutes later, with the books away, the computers powered down and everything locked up, Angela's husband arrived and had his arm solicitously around Angela.

Andy and Carly watched as he helped her into the car. They had carried her presents and put them in the boot. At the last minute Andy sneaked in his chocolates. Carly noted that Angela carried the angel.

"Have a good Christmas!" they both shouted as they drove away.

Then they were alone in the cold. Carly scuffed her boots in the frost while Andy seemed rooted to the spot.

"I should go," she muttered.

"Carly…" Andy said, liking the feel of her name on his tongue, "I was wondering

if you would like to go for a drink?"

Andy braced himself for the words *sorry I would love to but…*

"I'm sorry Andy, I would love to but… can I tell you a secret?" She stood on tiptoe and whispered. "I'm starving!"

"That's OK we can always go to a restaurant or something."

"Oh, I didn't mean that!" she replied, blushing. "I just meant a take-away."

"There's a good Malaysian take-away on Bothwell Street."

"That's my absolute favourite!"

"Really?" he asked, as they grinned at each other.

It had never occurred to either of them to appear disinterested – they were just too happy to do that – and later when Carly took Andy's arm and headed for the Snug Inn they thought about Angela.

"I do hope she's OK" said Carly.

"I'm sure she will be." Then added at the same time as Carly did, "She's a lovely person."

They started to laugh just for the sheer joy of it. After all it was Christmas.

Angela *was* OK. In fact she was glowing with robust health.

She ate one of Andy's chocolates as she looked at the angel. She really appreciated the gifts, but what she would appreciate more was if her two favourite customers got together.

It was strange but she had the feeling that they definitely would.

THE AUTHOR SAYS…

"I used to work in a library and was forever making up stories about my regulars. Pairing them up was a favourite pastime, hence the story."